DAMN THE SCHOOL SYSTEM—FULL SPEED AHEAD!

Damn the School System— Full Speed Ahead!

Vearl G. McBride

An Exposition-University Book
Exposition Press   New York

FIRST EDITION

© 1973 by Vearl G. McBride

LIBRARY OF CONGRESS CATALOG CARD NUMBER: 73-77585

SBN 0-682-47695-1

Manufactured in the United States of America
Published simultaneously in Canada by Transcanada Books

Contents

Contents

Preface

God bless those teachers and school administrators who are seriously trying to make some much needed changes in our schools. There are thousands of top-notch teachers and other school people who are really attempting some breakthroughs in their teaching. For these we should be sincerely grateful. But there are twice that many or more who are satisfied to remain as programmed robots, and who accept and repeat their mistakes. There are also some who are too lazy to change. Then there are those who are afraid to rock the boat for fear of losing their jobs. Well, jobs *are* scarce and hard to find.

Those teachers, administrators and parents who are fighting to make our schools the centers of learning that they should be are to be highly commended, and almost revered. But some of those teachers may lose their jobs if they are not careful and cautious. Only this day I spoke with a young, energetic teacher who has created many changes in her own classroom. She is "pushing" the children into "doing good works." And the children love it! But this teacher is spied upon by her colleague across the hall and her actions are reported to the principal. That worthy has called down the young innovator twice already for not following the prescription laid out for all the teachers.

When I asked her what she was going to do about it, she cupped both hands to her mouth and said in a loud whisper: "To———with that old biddy. I'm going to keep right on pushing my kids."

So I say, God bless *all* those fine and wonderful teachers dedicated to the proposition that children should be *taught,* not fraught with frustration.

And may that same God inspire the parents to *demand* of their school boards better administrators who will assume real educational leadership.

7

You parents, UP AND AT 'EM! A few weeks ago a mother of a sixth-grade boy called me on the telephone and begged me to help her son. She had just returned from a third visit with her boy's teacher and principal and was full of anger and frustration. They had told her again that the boy absolutely could not take home his reading textbook because it was against the school rules. She told me that she had asked them how the boy was "supposed to learn to read from his textbook if he is not allowed to read from it." "Academic oppressors," she called them. What else?!

I suggested that she go to the next higher authority—the superintendent. "What will happen to Jimmy if I do?" she asked. "What else *can* happen to him?" I responded. She agreed. As of this writing she has an appointment to see him. She is determined to raise a lot of h-e-double-q if necessary to get some rules changed. She is really incensed. If I may use her exact words: "These educational vampires are sucking my taxes right away from me while they let my boy go right down the drain."

More power to her and to the rest of you righteously indignant parents. UP AND AT 'EM!

V. G. McB.

DAMN THE SCHOOL SYSTEM—FULL SPEED AHEAD!

Chapter I

Damn the
Reading Teachers—
Full Speed Ahead

What this country needs is some Nader's Raiders in education. We don't have any right now, but if we are to improve
our schools, we're going to have to do some raiding. We'll have
to abolish some tenure laws and a lot of teachers along with
them. It isn't more money that we need. Money we've spent,
but it hasn't bought better schools; new and shinier equipment,
yes, but not better teaching. For this we need some raiders.
Maybe this book will help.

I am talking about the learning processes in general, and
about school subjects such as reading, math, spelling, and foreign
languages in particular. If our kids are really going to learn in
these areas, we are going to have to teach their teachers to teach
differently, or get rid of the teachers.

These are harsh words, but true words. This book will
pointedly point up what I mean, I hope. After twenty-six years
of teaching, fifteen of which have been spent in trying to educate
teachers, I have come to the conclusion that if we are to have
well-taught children who are to become tomorrow's responsible
adults, we will have to retrain our teachers or fire them. Failing
that, we will have to kick out scads of school boards and the
superintendents they employ, and get new ones. If we find that
we cannot do that, then our next alternative is to demand that
our school boards refuse to buy the unadulterated tripe being
sold by the many commercial companies which are in the business of selling children's textbooks, workbooks, and coloring
materials to the schools.

11

I feel that I can speak with some authority on this subject. Every year I visit some seventy-five elementary and secondary schoolrooms. I am not there to sell anything. I just watch teachers supposedly teaching children and young adults. Often I come away grinding my teeth in frustration and indignation and threatening to myself to quit the business of training young teachers. Then I become afraid to quit because, quite immodestly, I say to myself, "What will become of the educational system if I, or someone, doesn't keep pushing the novice teacher to do something different from what is being done in those classrooms?"

It is maddening to have to sit and watch teachers teach in the same manner I was taught forty-five years ago. "Oh," but you say, "the methods of teaching have changed a great deal since your time." Hogwash! Let me begin to show you what I mean.

Mrs. B. Elderberry has been teaching for twenty years. For the last ten years she has been teaching first grade. She has become an expert in traditional first-grade work. She divided her class into three reading groups; the high, the middle and the low. The two lowest groups use the same reading textbooks, but the middle group is ten pages ahead of the lowest group, and never the twain shall meet. The highest group, which the teacher enjoys very much, is in a different book, into which the middle group will someday graduate, but probably not the lowest group—not until next year, anyway.

The children in the high group are seated in a semicircle and are taking turns reading the story out loud. Each one reads a page, then it is the turn of the next child. The story is only four pages long and there are eight youngsters in the group. Each pupil "gets" to read twice. Perhaps there are fifteen words on a page. As the second reading begins (the children have already read the story silently, so in reality this is the third reading), the youngsters begin to lose interest. The teacher sparks it up by asking some questions she has been directed to ask by the authors of the textbook. She is using the invaluable Guidebook, which only the teacher may see. The children's attention wanders.

They've been over this stuff before. Billy's pet turtle was interesting at first, but not again and again. In the group Joe pinches Chuck, and Chuck responds just as Joe hoped he would. They both gain the teacher's attention and are hushed. The teacher is bored too, and is engaged from time to time in studying and picking at the lacquer on her finger nails.

Some questions from the teacher with the pupils responding. The teacher tries to bring out certain points in the lesson. She even tries to have the children relate to the story. The children finish the lesson and are given the next day's assignment. They then return the books to the bookshelf where they are kept until the next lesson.

They are not allowed to keep the books in their desks because they might want to read that next story, or one farther on in the book, *before* the next reading session. The Guidebook, the principal, and the teacher are dead set against that happening. Why? "Well," they tell you, "if a child reads ahead in his book, he will be bored and inattentive when the group gets to that part."

Inattentive my foot! After a kid has read something three times he is already bored and restless. And he has to sit and listen to a bunch of others who are just as bored as he and who can't read the stuff well enough to make good sense out of it. And does it make good sense with the *best* reader droning through such tripe as, "See Mike ride." "Mary, see Mike ride." "Mike and Mary, look at Jeff." Really exciting stuff.

Let's return to that high group that just finished its reading lesson. The youngsters now return to their seats and, having picked up their workbooks from the shelves, begin to fill in the blanks relating to the story they have just read. They make X's on pictures, draw lines around words and pictures, and draw connecting lines between words and/or pictures. They devote much more time to these activities than they do to actual reading. The lack of enthusiasm is plainly expressed on their faces.

How much reading have they learned? Well, they were only supposed to learn three new words this day. That is all the

Guidebook called for. No teacher with good sense will disturb the principal and jeopardize her own job by going beyond what the sacred Guidebook dictates.

A student teacher once had the temerity to suggest to the supervising teacher that perhaps they could have *two* stories in one day, and have *six* new words. Unthinkable! After some rather vigorous remarks, the supervising teacher explained that "we have only so many books, and we have to make them last all year." She went on to say that she had been teaching in that school for twenty years, and had survived eight school principals. "I found that it is good policy to simply follow the instructions given in the Guidebook. If you do that, you won't get in any trouble."

That seemed to end the matter. You just do not buck City Hall. I think the saddest thing about it all was that the student teacher finally came to believe it. And what of the poor kids? Who cares? They were happy in their ignorance. They didn't know that they almost had a chance to learn twice as much in one day as they usually learned. When we remember that this kind of thing is happening in thousands of classrooms all over the nation, we ought to shudder. We no longer need to wonder why nearly half our students fail in school because they cannot read well enough to do the work required of them. We are not truly teaching them to read. We are teaching them how to draw lines and circles and to make X's.

Meanwhile, back at the ranch, the middle and low groups are having gobs of un-fun. While that high group has been in the barbership reading circle (that's where the teacher says "next," as each child finishes reading aloud his part), the other two groups have been at their seats doing some exciting things. They have been coloring ducks, rabbits, or something similar, and in general wasting their time. I know whereof I speak. I have sat in these rooms hundreds of times and have actually recorded some of the activities in which these youngsters have engaged. Sometimes they do some number work, or spell a word or two, or write their names. But it's an aimless sort of thing, with a great deal of wandering around on the part of the children, with many interruptions and pauses in whatever they are doing.

Each of the two lower groups finally gets its turn with the teacher. They have to go slower, and often they do not finish their stories in one day, so they sometimes take two days to learn three words. The teacher is bored to death, and so are the kids. I have been told by scores of teachers that these children simply can't go any faster. Yet everybody knows that these same kids can learn gobs of things on TV, or at play, etc. Why not in the classroom?

I know why, and so do you. If your child, from the day he was born until he reaches school age, were to have heard only a few words a day, he would not have learned to speak, probably. He actually encountered thousands of words everyday of his life. If he is anywhere near normal, he *has* to learn to talk. You would have a difficult time keeping him from learning under those conditions. He becomes a whiz at many things at home, then he becomes six and enters the first grade. Halt! His learning slows down and often comes to a screeching halt. He might have a speaking and hearing vocabulary of fifteen thousand to twenty-five thousand words. But now he is in school and doesn't know much, so he gets only a few words a day in his reading. He has had a whole year in kindergarten of getting "ready to read," (some more hogwash). But now he cannot read, and in order to keep him from learning to read, we expertly give him less and less of what he needs most.

Today my own first-grader came home full of delight. We asked her why. She said there were three things taking place tomorrow: Her big brother is coming home from college, her class is going to the library, and they are going to have ice cream for lunch. All three things in one day! Now, my first-grade daughter is a good reader and loves to go to the library. Her class is only allowed to go there once a week for thirty minutes, and tomorrow was to be that day! She would get to check out one book. She could read that book before her class leaves the library, but she will not do that, "because the teacher will be mad at me if I do," she says. She doesn't know it, but the librarian will also

be mad at her if she does. I have talked with the librarian about
it, and she insists that no child can read more than one book a
week at the age of six.

My three youngest children learned to read before they entered kindergarten, and were even told that they should not
learn to read until the first grade. All of their kindergarten teachers told them that "in kindergarten we get ready to read. We do
not learn to read until first grade. Tell your parents that." So all
of them forgot how to read during that year of "getting ready"
to read. You see, the children believed their teachers, and even
told us that they were not *supposed* to read yet. In order to support their teachers and the school, we did not push them in the
reading effort that we so wanted to do. DTSS—FSA!!

My present six-year-old reads choppily aloud. Words such
as little become lit-tle, and running becomes run-ning. This is the
way they read in their circle at school. But at home, she reads
silently at around 400-450 words a minute. That is why she can
read her library book in less than thirty minutes. But in school
if she reads that fast, her teacher gets after her and tells her to
"stay with the rest of the class." So at school she reads about 50
words a minute, which is average for first-graders. She has no
desire to get the teacher mad at her.

You ask, "How can she read that fast?" It's because I taught
her how to in the summer between her kindergarten and first
grade. She loves it. All of my other children are also fast readers.
(I have seven, so this should make me some kind of authority
on children.) I taught them, also. It isn't hard. Just tell them
they can, then give them the opportunity, and they will read
circles around most adults. You have to do something about eye
movement patterns, etc., too. But these will be discussed later.

Do you begin to see why I said that we teach reading in the
schools about the same as we did forty years ago? I look in vain
for new ideas which are supposed to be presented by our reading
experts. I find none. Companies which publish children's textbooks will, from time to time, ballyhoo in a loud voice that they
have a brand new reading program to present to our nation's
schools. They then go about convincing an unsuspecting public

that it had better buy that program or our children will sure enough be doomed to failure in their schoolwork. It is quite likely that our kids are doomed to failure, but certainly not because we do not buy this new product. For if we give even a cursory look at the product, we find that it contains new stories and new pictures, perhaps even more pictures, but nothing new about techniques, methods, philosophies, etc. *I challenge you to find any of these in the scores of series published today.*

You say you challenge *me* to show *you* the truth of what I have just said? I'm glad you said that! Look here:

Recently a group of my prospective teachers, interested in finding new ways to teach reading, observed and took notes in thirty-six classrooms in nine schools. The classrooms contained children in grades three through six. What did they find? You won't believe this, but it's the truth. *The average number of pages read in the reading textbooks in these thirty-six classes in six weeks was a little less than two pages a day!* The highest number of pages read in any one room was eleven pages in one week, or slightly over two pages a day on the average.

These kids had reading classes everyday. What do you suppose they were doing during the reading periods if they were not reading? They were doing just what most of the kids have been doing for years and years, at least during my lifetime. They were working in their glorious workbooks in which they drew lines under words, circles around words, writing down words that had the same initial consonant blends, writing answers to questions in the workbook, breaking words into syllables, etc.

In short, the youngsters were becoming experts in drawing lines and circles, copying words in workbooks; but becoming experts in reading they were not.

One of the teachers interviewed about this expressed supreme disgust with what she was doing in this way: "Look, I have to teach this way to keep my job. I'm bored to death with it and so are the kids, but I have to do it because I'm supposed to keep right along with the teacher across the hall, so what else can I do?" We said among ourselves later: "Get the heck out of there or else do something worthwhile."

Do you still wonder why our kids are not learning to read?

But I guess it is not all the fault of the teachers. The principal of that school—a "modern" school, newly built—said to one of my students who was visiting there, "We don't particularly care for new ideas or innovations here. We're trying to maintain a status quo so that all of the children can progress at the same rate." How's that for progress? He has been principal in that school system for twenty years, and is considered one of the better administrators. I can tell you this: He is a clean one. I saw him jerk a kid up by the hair when the boy threw a wad of paper along the hallway, not knowing that there was an eagle eye on him.

In one of the schools where my students were observing, they were watching a fourth-grade reading class in session. Afterwards, one of them asked the teacher how many reading textbooks the children would use that school year. "This is it," said the teacher, tapping the one in her hand. Think of it! It will take those kids nine months to read one book! That, I submit, is mighty slow reading.

Later, we had occasion to check the number of pages in that particular book. There were 315 pages. Consider a school year of 180 days, and do some dividing, and you find that those kids were taking a whole school year to read one book because they were reading *less* than two pages a day.

Do you still wonder why our kids are not learning to read?

It is time to do some contrasting. There are remedies which are being put into effect gradually. Now, I want you to believe what I am going to tell you because it's the truth.

I get downright mad (angry, too!) at schools and teachers and publishing companies when I think how they are bilking our children out of learning. You would, too, if you had seen the things that I have seen, and that I have done. Sometimes, I stand in open-mouthed amazement as I watch kids (and adults) perform. In a small town in Missouri, for example, there is a kindergarten class which is doing things never before performed by a group this age. The children are learning to read rapidly. Some of them can read as high as *two thousand* words a minute:

and with understanding. They are doing things that most adults can't do. Here is a group of thirteen children who are not even supposed to be taught reading, many so-called authorities say. When my daughter was in kindergarten, the teacher told me that she was not allowed to teach the children to read. The majority of school systems are the same in this respect. Someone has sold them on the idea that they are not supposed to teach kindergarten children to read.

But the teacher in the small town in Missouri is not only teaching her children to read, but to read *rapidly*—and they love it! I visited there recently, and when the teacher announced that it was time for "our speed reading class," the kids ran screaming with delight to get their books. They literally fell over each other in their excitement. One would have thought that the teacher had announced recess. Then they read. It was pure joy to watch those youngsters perform. They've been taught rapid reading from the beginning, so they do not even know what slow reading is. Nor will they ever know unless some stupid teacher teaches them to read slowly, or tries to *make* them read slowly.

The following incident happened just the other day in what is supposed to be a "modern and progressive" school. A sixth-grade girl who had taken private lessons in rapid reading and had given several public demonstrations of her ability, now has a teacher who refuses to "allow that kind of thing in *my* class." The teacher assigned the class a given lesson to read and warned the girl not to "speed read." In the twenty-minute period, which the class had to read the assignment, the girl read it thirty-three times. However, she did not tell the teacher she had done so. She had no wish to bring down the wrath of the teacher upon her. *Think how much more this girl, and others like her, could learn if we would allow them to do so!* Truly, we are "plumb dumb."

Then consider the fourth-grade teacher who, on the sly, and without letting her principal know about it, has taught her fourth-graders to read at high speeds. The mother of one of these fourth-graders told me that her son "reads a book before breakfast every morning." Before he had learned to read fast, she said, she almost had to beat him to get him to read anything. "I have only one criticism of that teacher," the mother said. "She's making a bookworm out of my boy—and he loves it."

Contrast this situation with that of an ignorant teacher who threatened to send one of *her* fourth-grade boys to the principal's office if he didn't quit reading faster than the others in the class. It's the truth! She actually told the boy that. But, she had given him, "fair warning." She had reprimanded him several times for finishing the story so much ahead of the others in the class. Now she was threatening *real* punishment if he did not quit learning so fast!

You think this is far-fetched? A mother asked her daughter's fifth-grade teacher what he thought of the child taking a course in rapid reading. To which the teacher replied: "Don't let her do that. Your child will go crazy if she reads too fast." This sounds like the advice of a witch doctor. How could anyone be so downright ignorant? Quite obviously, the teacher knew nothing of what is involved in rapid reading. But it was double trouble because the mother believed him and did not enroll the child at that time. Two years later she allowed the girl to "try out" speed reading, and now deeply regrets the loss of the two years. She also castigates the teacher and herself for their lack of knowledge. The child reads ten times faster and is a much better student.

I won't tell you how fast a bunch of second-graders can read because it's hard to believe, but the truth is that they can read so fast that they finished all of their books before Thanksgiving and the teacher had to request additional funds for new books. She didn't get them until after Christmas, so she had to have the class go through the old ones again, which they did. It was terribly boring to many of the youngsters, but others didn't mind. The teacher seriously questioned what they learned from "the warmed-over stuff."

What did the kids think of the fast reading? They came early and wanted to stay late to "read that way." They loved it, and so did the teacher. It made for some exciting times, and the kids learned fast and much more than the second-graders across the hall. That's what school is all about—learning, I mean.

Compare these kids with another group of second-graders I saw. I walked into the classroom as one of the reading groups was having its turn at the reading corner. As I watched each child take his turn at reading monotonously aloud, I saw the teacher poke the little boy sitting next to her from time to time. I noticed that he did not have a book, but the others did, and when it came his turn to read aloud, the teacher would let him look on hers.

When the opportunity presented itself, I asked the teacher about him. "Well," she exclaimed, "that little devil; he reads ahead in his lesson, and reads the next story. Then when the group gets to that place, he's bored and starts fidgeting. So, I just took the book away from him and wouldn't let him read at all."

Man, what a sure way to keep a boy from learning to read! It will work every time, if that's what we're aiming at. This teacher seemed to be doing just that. But she was not alone in this kind of stupidity. Consider the student teacher who had the audacity to allow one of her third-grade pupils to read the next story in the reader the day before his reading group got to that story in the book. She was gently reprimanded by her supervising teacher. Then it happened again, but this time the student teacher did something completely inexcusable. She allowed a child *to take home his reader!* The child liked to read and told the student teacher that he didn't have any books at home. The young teacher happened to know something about the boy's family and knew he was speaking the truth, so she let him. Result: The student teacher was called into the principal's office and was told that this time her misdemeanor would be overlooked, but that she was not to let such a thing happen again. If she could not abide by the rules, she would have to find another school in which to do her student teaching. What did she do? She abided. She wanted to get a good recommendation from her school. She had to have a job. What about the child who wanted to read? That was not the important thing, apparently; the important thing was to follow the rules.

Then there was the new teacher whose principal learned that

she was letting the children in the first grade read more than one lesson or story a day, and teaching them to read rapidly. "You follow the Guidebook if you want to stay in this school," commanded the principal. She did want to stay, and she followed the Guidebook. But the "damage" had already been done. Her first-graders could already read up to 1,250 words a minute. The average rate in her class was 500 words a minute, and the average comprehension was 86 percent. The other two sections of the first grade in that school averaged 55 words a minute, with 69 and 73 percent comprehension on the same tests administered to all three sections. What did the principal do when he saw the results of the tests? Nothing. The school had paid for these materials (guidebooks and workbooks) and they were to be used as indicated. The kids had to go through them again.

Who indicated how they were to be used? The textbook writers and publishers, of course. And the schools, after paying out good money for the stuff, as the principal above indicated, feel they have to use it, and use it they do. Two fourth-grade teachers told me a short time ago that "After all, the people who write these books *are* experts and should know what they are doing, and we feel we should follow their suggestions." And these are ladies who have been teaching for twenty to twenty-five years. Well, anyway, they've taught one year twenty-five times.

It appears that a few textbook writers have brought us to our knees in this field of reading. And I don't mean that they've brought us to our knees in prayer, but maybe that's where we need to go. These writers tell the teachers what to teach and when to teach what. "Oh, pshaw, that's not so," you say, and the teachers rise defensively to say the same. Oh yeah, just look! Here are some directions given in the Teachers' Guidebooks which accompany the reading textbooks of five well-known publishing companies:

"The teachers work with the pupils on all lessons." (None may work by himself.)

"The books should not be kept in the pupil's desks. They should be distributed just before each work period begins and collected as soon as a lesson is completed and checked." (Has anyone ever devised a better way to keep children from reading?) Chain the Bible to the pulpit!

The . . . (workbook) should be in the hands of the pupils *only* when the pages are being marked or discussed." (No independent work allowed.)

"As each exercise is designed to parallel the work in the text, the exercises should not be used out of sequence. Each page of the Workbook should be used at the point indicated in this manual." (No child must move ahead of the others. We stay together.)

"What skills are to be taught and the order in which they are to be taught have been built into the storybook and the accompanying workbook." (Notice: We will tell you what to teach and when to teach it.)

"At the beginning of each plan the teachers are given the pages of the storybook and the study book to use the new words." (Don't rock the boat by trying something on your own.)

My own children have reading books that are passed out each day and gathered up at the end of the reading period each time. They are not allowed to keep their books in their desks, nor are they allowed to bring them home. Do you know why? It's because they might *read* them.

Now, I submit that the reading textbook was designed, theoretically, at least, to help a child learn to read, but if he is not allowed to read it for enjoyment, how can he possibly learn to read? The president of the United States and the United States commissioner of education have declared us to be a nation of poor readers. Is it any wonder that we are in this sad situation? How could we have devised a better way to make us poorer readers than what we have? A newspaper writer recently said in his column that if the president is going to succeed in his "right-to-read" program, it will only be over the dead bodies of the teachers who teach reading. Amen and amen.

I have yet to find a textbook designed for the elementary or high school (indeed, how many reading textbooks can *anyone* find designed for high schools) which even hints that these kids can read any faster than their parents could, or should. I wonder why nothing is said in these books about the possibility of one's developing the ability to read a few thousand words a minute.

A superintendent of schools recently told me that his daughter had read 240 books last spring. She had taken a special course in rapid reading and had developed into a very fast reader. So it was that she was able to read the 240 books with some ease. Now I ask, why do the textbook writers avoid as with a passion any mention of this kind of possibility on the part of the pupils? We have irrefutable evidence that rapid reading, hence rapid learning, is a reality. Such evidence has been presented to several book companies on various occasions, but they have chosen not to use the evidence. It was not because they were not interested, they said, but rather because they were already committed to a few million dollars worth of other programs and, of course, could not change then. I wouldn't want to lose a million dollars if I had it, either.

In the meantime, however, our children continue to suffer in abysmal ignorance. Again, a case in point. I walked into a second-grade classroom to observe a student teacher. She was over in one corner of the room partially hidden behind a screen, working with five children on sounds and directions. They were seated at a table, with each child using a set of earphones while he listened to a sweet voice on a recording giving directions concerning the marking of X's on certain vowel letters. Plenty of time was given by the voice for the marking of the X's, and in the meantime the children looked at me, at each other, or just sat and stared. Then the voice would come on again.

This went on for ten minutes. Then the student teacher, following the instructions of the supervising teacher, checked the papers and complimented each child on his efforts. How did the children do on this assignment? Wonderfully well! Not one child missed one sound. All had their X's in just the right places. Now, what does this mean? Does it mean that the children were learning sounds? Maybe. But the fact that they got them all right might mean that this particular activity was a complete waste of time for these kids. They would have been much better off with something more challenging, more stimulating and more fun.

That is not all there is to this story. I learned that the student teacher was doing the same thing with every child in the room in groups of five. I inquired gently of the young teacher and her supervisor about *all* of the children needing this kind of thing, and both assured me that they all did need it. I did not argue with them, of course. I was not there to tell the supervising teacher how to teach, but, when I got the student teacher out to one side, I questioned her about it, and she whispered to me that she, frankly, thought it was a dumb thing to do, but she had to do it. It's true; she was supposed to be learning under this experienced teacher even, I suppose, the things *not* to do.

These kids were engaged in a slow, tedious way of learning to read, and what were they actually learning? Well, they learned how to make pretty X's. But they already knew their vowel sounds. Now it is true that there were probably some of those second-graders who did not know their vowel sounds, but may I point out again that if they do not know something, the best way to have them learn it is to give them much of what they don't know instead of just a wee dose.

The best way to learn to read is to *read*. We do *not* learn to read, nor to do anything else, by going slowly around Robin Hood's barn to get at something. You see, this was a daily exercise for all of the kids in that room, whether they needed it or not. The five I observed definitely did *not* need this activity, but they got it anyway. I felt sorry for them; but they had to use that equipment. It cost a lot of money.

I want you to compare these second-graders with those youngsters in that other second grade where the kids went through all of their books before Thanksgiving. Who learned more? Who had more fun? Reading, like anything else, must be an enjoyable experience to be effective. Those children who read scads of books *had* to become better readers than those in that grade where they were slowly making the X's. They had to learn more because they were encountering more, and experiencing more. Surely this does make sense, does it not?

Sometimes it seems that outright stupidity exists in our schools. Look again at that teacher who was giving her first-grade pupils three new words a day. If I were going to try to learn to be a car mechanic, would I be given just three small tasks to learn in one day? What utter foolishness! And those second-graders who were making X's—how long do you suppose it will take them to really learn to read?

A high-ranking member of the recently formed National Council for the Disadvantaged made the following remark: "I believe that every child who enters school becomes disadvantaged." In other words, teach your child all you possibly can before he begins school, because as soon as he enters school, he begins to lose. Those kids making X's certainly were losing. Those children who learned to read before they entered kindergarten lost a whole year! This makes me so mad every time I think of it, I could throw rocks at some people. Blast them!

Probably the greatest failure in all of our educational system is the failure to teach reading. The percentage of poor readers and nonreaders is increasing every year. Cities like Chicago and New York double their budgets and institute new (so-called) programs to improve the reading ability of their students. Still the results of reading tests continue to show a downward trend. In nearly every college in the country, there are special classes where reading improvement is taught. Yet the professors of English complain that the students cannot write decent papers because they cannot read.

In his message to Congress in 1970, President Nixon said:

> We now spend more than $1 billion a year for educational programs run under Title I of the Elementary Act. Most of these have stressed the teaching of reading, but before and after tests suggest that only nineteen percent of the children in such programs improve their reading significantly; fifteen percent appear to fall behind more than expected; and more than two-thirds of the children remain unaffected—that is, they continue to fall behind.

Now, I want you to pay close attention to this next part, and let's do some cold, calculating reasoning together. Our nation is in poor condition reading-wise. Since the president's "right-to-read program" has gone into effect, we have spent even more than the $1 billion mentioned by Mr. Nixon as having been spent in 1969. What's going on here, anyway? Let's see:

ITEM: Colleges supposedly teach teachers how to teach reading.

ITEM: The student teacher goes into the classroom where he is to do his student teaching, and begins to observe his supervising teacher. He notes the materials and techniques used by his supervisor.

ITEM: He is "given" a reading class to teach. He uses the same materials and techniques used by his supervisor. This is a must.

ITEM: The materials he uses have been purchased by the school.

ITEM: The company published the information written by the textbook writers.

ITEM: The student teacher follows the instructions given in the Guidebook.

ITEM: This is what he has observed the supervising teacher do. It is the supervising teacher's classroom. The student teacher does what he is told. He follows the instructions as commanded.

ITEM: The student teacher graduates and gets a job as a teacher.

ITEM: He teaches the way he was told to teach. He uses the materials given him, and which were purchased by the school from the publishing companies.

ITEM: He follows the instructions as written by the textbook authors and published by the companies.

ITEM: He is required to do so.

ITEM: Eighty-one percent of the children do not learn how to read well enough to succeed in school or out of school. They are only mediocre or less.

ITEM: Who is to blame?

ITEM: The people who write and publish children's textbooks. They tell the teachers what to teach, how to teach, and when to teach what. The school administrators support the companies in this and coerce the teachers into the same kind of support.

We can see this kind of thing reflected again and again. I went into a third-grade classroom one morning where a student teacher was at work. Everything was nice and quiet. The young teacher whispered to me to please be seated, that the children were doing "pre-reading." I didn't know exactly what that meant, but it was obvious that I wasn't supposed to talk, so I sat in the designated chair and didn't talk. I just sat and looked at my watch from time to time. The children were reading something. Finally one of them finished apparently, looked up, looked at me, grinned, and looked around at the others who were still reading. In a moment or two, another finished, etc. These children whispered among themselves a bit, until shushed by the student teacher, then began busying themselves in one way or another. Some just sat, one sharpened his pencil until stopped by the student teacher, and others looked out the window, etc.

Finally, it appeared, all of the children had completed their reading silently, and the student teacher, in a very bright and enthusiastic voice (her college supervisor was there, you see), told the children to bring their books and their chairs to the reading center.

Exactly thirteen minutes had elapsed from the time I sat down in that chair until the young teacher ordered the children to the reading center. How long they had been reading before I came in I do not know, but some of the children sat for seven to ten minutes with absolutely nothing to do while the rest of the group was finishing the story they had been assigned.

I thought to myself, this kind of thing is being repeated thousands of times with hundreds of thousands of children everyday. What a terrible, stupid waste of brain power! But this is what is ordered by the writers and the publishers, and by the school administrators and the teachers. This is often considered "good teaching." Remember the experienced teacher who told her student teacher "to follow the rules"? That experienced teacher had kept her job these many years by following the rules.

As for grouping, let's blast it out of the schools. It is a heinous practice which has been perpetuated by the sellers of textbooks because it helps to sell. The only way really, to teach effectively all of the children in the room to read, is to group them "according to ability," they say. Poppycock, baloney, and stuff like that! They are just plain out-and-out lying. *This practice of grouping is carried on in about 98 percent of the schools in this country, and 81 percent of the kids are failing because of it and its resulting evils.* We had better open our eyes to the truth of the matter. We ought to get smart and kick out those school people who are not imaginative enough to do something different. There *are* other and better ways to teach kids to read.

I won't go into the usual pros and cons concerning grouping except to say that it is unfair, can be emotionally upsetting to a child, and in general does not help kids to learn to read. Despite the fact that its proponents have failed to demonstrate the superiority of grouping over nongrouping, the foul practice continues in the majority of our elementary schools and in many junior and senior high schools. The thing that we must do is to take a closer look at what the individual does as he reads. It is *he* about whom we are concerned, not the group. Only the individual is important. We might think we teach groups, but only the individual learns, so let us concentrate on him.

First, how does he see? I have asked this question many times in my classes of prospective teachers and often have received the answer, "With his eyes." Remarkable! But does he see with his *eyes* or with his *eye?* Many of us know that we see better with one eye than we do with the other. What we do not realize, sometimes, is that often we see with only one eye because the other is "resting." The brain "mothers" the eyes and sometimes allows one to rest while the other does the work. Unfortunately, the "mothering" usually is done in favor of the same eye most of the time, hence the mothered eye becomes a little weaker and the working eye becomes a little stronger.

What does this mean for the child who is learning to read? Well, it might mean a lot to him, but it usually doesn't take him anywhere. That's because the teacher knows nothing about this kind of thing. It is not even hinted at in the sacred Guidebook; therefore, it is ignored by the teacher, or by most teachers. I must add hurriedly that there are many, many teachers who are very much concerned about the eyesight of the children in their classrooms, but very few who understand and do anything about this problem. The school principal is often the hardest one to get around. What the teacher is able to do in this respect is often dictated by the "wisdom" of the principal.

Let me illustrate. Here is part of a letter which I received from a teacher who was at the same time a student in one of my extension classes. I don't want to get her into further hot water with her principal, so I will not give her name.

Feb. 5, 19—

Dear Dr. McBride:

You asked me to write to you about the little boy I had in my first grade class. Remember, he was the one who could read upside down and also wrote upside down.

Do I have something to tell and I am still seeing red about about it! They finally got him in at ———— City on Feb. 8. Can you imagine this? (He had been referred the previous September). He is farsighted and was wearing nearsighted glasses. The place where he had gotten his glasses has since gone out of business and I can see why.

They have taken the old glasses from him now and said they might have to give him glasses to read with. At first he would almost shut his eyes when he read, but his eyes are apparently adjusting because he's no longer doing this. He wasn't able to print on the line either, but now he is. This was worse later in the day when his eyes became more tired. . . .

I am grateful that I discovered this when I did, but still some damage was certainly done. He really is doing pretty good in his school work now.

Sincerely,

Mrs. E. N.

P.S. My principal thought I was too overly concerned about my boy with the eye problem, and still thinks so.

Certainly not all school principals are as stupid as this one is, but there are far too many like him infesting our schools.

The teacher's responsibility in this matter of the child's vision is most important. He must make sure that the pupil is seeing with both eyes and that his reading material is placed in such a position as to take advantage of that child's particular manner of seeing. That is, from what angle or angles does he see best? (This kind of thing is not even hinted at in the Guidebook.) It has been assumed in the past that there are two ways to hold a book, i.e., either flat on a more or less flat surface, or by standing it on its lower edge and slanting it slightly away from us. Why have we assumed this? I don't know, but we just have, and that seems to be reason enough to continue it, but that's really not good enough. There are better things in store for us.

As a matter of fact, there is nothing at all wrong with holding the reading material in either or both of those positions at various times *if these are the best ways for the individual.* Many people, including children, can see the material better and can read faster and understand more if they hold the book or other reading matter in some psoition other than the two to which most of us are presently confined.

In my reading classes over the past eighteen years, I have found that there are always several in each class who are able to read better with their materials tilted or slanted in some direction other than the two traditional ones mentioned above. The direction and the degree of the tilt, or the slant, should be left up to the individual to determine for himself. No one can or should tell him how it is to be done. The important thing is for the teacher to be aware of these possibilities and encourage each pupil to experiment with the way or ways he can see and read best.

Never will I forget that gorgeous young creature (a first-grade teacher) who stood in front of her class one day and with a beautiful smile and happy voice said: "All right boys and girls, get ready to read your books. Everyone sit up straight, feet flat on the floor, books straight in front of you." I didn't ask that teacher how long she expected the kids to maintain that military-like posture. I wasn't there to tell her how to teach her class, but I sure got after the student teacher who was working under her, and gave her the very devil when she told me that she felt the children had to learn that kind of discipline. I told her I thought the children were to learn to read and to enjoy the process. She flushed, and she said she guessed that was right. I reminded her that certainly that was not the position in which *she* enjoyed reading, and she readily agreed.

Many of our present-day reading practices are difficult, if not impossible, to justify if we assert that it is the individual in whom we are interested. Again I use an illustration, hot off the stove, to point up our padlocked learning situation.

I was visiting one of my student teachers in the third grade. Again, a reading class was in progress and the children were seated in a circle with the student teacher a part of the circle. Apparently it was "Billy's group," and Billy had already gone to the shelf where the reading books are kept and had passed them to the members of the group. The young teacher saw that each child had a copy of the book, then said: "All right [she always started that way because it seemed to give her a couple of seconds to gauge and control her voice, and besides, her college supervisor was there and she was a bit nervous], everyone sit up straight [rigid spines while reading, you see] with feet flat on the floor; heads up!"

After some discussion about the new words which were to be encountered (there were five of them), each child was given a "turn" at reading aloud from a prescribed story. Each read carefully and often slowly in order that the words could be pronounced correctly. After the completion of the story, or after each child had had an opportunity to read, and the story had been discussed at length, the books were gathered up and Billy's group members went back to their seats and another group assembled for their turn in the reading corner.

When I got a chance to talk with the student teacher, I asked her if all of the children in Billy's group could read equally well from the book they were using. (The teacher was bright-eyed and smiling for she felt that she and the children had performed well in front of the college supervisor.) It was obvious that Billy's group was the lowest of the three groups in the room. "Well, no," she said, "but we just can't have more than three groups because we don't really have enough time as it is, and anyway, they will all learn a little bit just from hearing the others read. Some of the children just are not ready for reading. They really shouldn't be in this grade at all. I can't understand why the teacher of last year even promoted them or the teacher the year before. My supervising teacher here has already talked with the principal about the situation. I hope something will be done about it. She says that absolutely no child is going to leave *this* grade without knowing how to read." So *there!*

I asked my young trainee about the books for the other two groups and was assured that each pupil in a given group read from a copy of the assigned book for his group. The sweet and so very knowledgeable young teacher continued: "Of course, there are one or two, and maybe three, in each group that have a hard time reading from their books because they don't know all of the words, but my supervisor feels they just don't really try. I think if they *would* try harder, they could get it all right."

We got to talking about special help for some of those kids, and the student teacher was quick to fill me in on how good and attentive she was to the children's needs: "Oh, my teacher and I get here early as often as we can and help some of the slower ones. Of course, the children who need the help most don't always come early. They would rather play outside most of the time. [Well, what do you know!] We try to give the faster pupils more advanced work, but when we have so many youngsters in the room, it's hard to give them very much special attention."

The situation I have just described is not a bit unusual. It is repeated thousands of times daily in our schools. It is often *not* the individual who is receiving the focus of attention. It is "Billy's *group*." Again, we must not be concerned about the *group;* it is only the individual who learns. His needs cannot be met when he receives the same treatment as the group. The group does not have a specified vision problem, hearing problem, comprehension or response problem. This type of specificity is found only in the individual person. In the majority of our schools, that person is being left out. He is, confound it, simply a second-class or third-class citizen. And you and I had better do something about it or we'll be met at the Judgment Bar by someone with a pitchfork!

Chapter II

How to Read
Shockingly Fast

The 1965 White House Conference on Youth severely criticized educators for the lack of innovations in education. Somebody certainly needed, and needs, to castigate them. Too often we are a bunch of duds. One mother recently said: "What we need to do is to educate the educators. They are the *most* uneducable of us all."

There was a vivid illustration of this recently at a reading symposium, and an illustration also of how desperately teachers and parents really *do* want something better than we have been getting. Each of the five members of the symposium panel was supposed to take fifteen minutes to present his subject. Each of the first four droned on in the same manner, offering the same suggestions that have been offered in nearly every book on the teaching of reading for the past ten or fifteen years.

It came the turn of the fifth and last speaker and he could see that many in the audience had settled down for a good nap. They were sure they would hear more of the same. They didn't. In less than a minute they were wide-awake and listening with interest and delight. The speaker was outlining some new ideas, things that a few of the people in the audience had heard about vaguely, and that some had never heard about at all. After the meeting the teachers and parents surged around that speaker begging for more information about the things he had presented. It was really embarrassing to the speaker because his colleagues on the panel were left standing by themselves.

What had the speaker said that brought such an enthusiastic response from a heretofore uninterested audience? Among other things, he had told them about that second grade which had run out of books by Thanksgiving, and about those kindergarten children who were being taught to read rapidly. He had told them of a group of first-graders who were being given instruction in rapid reading. Some of them could read as high as three thousand words a minute with understanding. And he had told them of second-graders who could read so fast that he was afraid to tell the truth about them for fear of being called a big liar. He told them briefly how the teachers of all of these kids had taught them to "lie" to their parents and to tell them of great speeds in reading to which they were attaining. But then the parents came to see and stayed to see more of this phenomenon.

He described so-called "remedial" cases which had blossomed under this new kind of instruction. He told them how children who had been poor readers and poor "spellers" had been given hundreds of words weekly in spelling and thousands of words weekly in reading, and how these youngsters had "eaten them up" and had asked for more! The same had been true of mathematics. The speaker told of how they had given classes of children up to five hundred math problems a week, and how the children insisted that the special math teacher remain in the room up to the very last *second*. In both the spelling and math classes, the children asked for more words and problems, but the teachers simply could not prepare more than six hundred spelling words a week!

But now, how? How did these youngsters learn to read rapidly, and to spell and do math problems at rates of five hundred and six hundred a week? And how did that second-grade teacher get those kids through all their books by Thanksgiving? Well, I'll tell you if you will promise not to call me a liar. I don't mind being called a liar if I'm telling a lie, but I don't like to be called one when I'm *not* lying, and in this book I have told the truth, so here is *how to read faster and have more fun!*

We have been taught, quite thoroughly, to read one word at a time. This we had drilled into us in the first grade and in the following years. In about the fifth or sixth grade, actual instruction in *how* to read ceased because it was assumed, I suppose, that by that time we had all learned to read (the mistake of the century!). We have continued to read just as we were taught in the early grades, reading slowly and saying each word in our minds. (We were taught arithmetic in the same stupid way, and also spelling.)

Of course, it was necessary in the beginning instruction in reading to teach the children the left-to-right concept, mainly because that is the way we write, but in the process the fact was overlooked that not all of us can see *best* in reading from left to right. Nothing was said (and I do mean *nothing!*) about the possibility that some children might have a wider span of vision than others and can see much more than one or two or three words at a time. The way most of us now read, i.e., from left to right then sweeping back (the return sweep), is really an odd, unusual, and peculiar way of seeing. In no other "seeing" activity do we see as we are taught to see in reading. When we look at the scenes around us, when we look at pictures, or when we are driving along the highway, etc., we do not use this manner of seeing. Why, then, have we insisted on it in reading? The answer comes immediately: "Well, that's the way the words go." True, but we do not *think* from left to right, do we? There is much more to be said about this kind of thing, but let us go on, and shortly you will see what I mean.

I must inject another thought at this point before going into the precise techniques of learning to read rapidly. Scientists are still studying the phenomenon of light and vision. No one knows *why* we see. We know the *mechanisms* that transmit the messages from the eyes to the brain, but we do not know *why* all of this takes place. We know that an object might be seen better from one angle than from another by one person, while a second person will see it better from quite a different angle. Furthermore, many of us *like* to look at some things from different angles or positions from what others do.

Interestingly, we have never applied this kind of thing to the teaching of reading until recently. *The angle of vision in reading* becomes a highly significant factor for each individual because of the differences which exist in us all. I must suggest here the possibility that the angle at which the light enters the eyes and its subsequent contact with the retina, and the later impulse(s) carried by the optic nerves to the brain, might prove to be of invaluable help to us. We know that the brain responds to different stimuli in different ways, even to the shading of light. The process by which the individual receives messages from the printed page is mysterious. Sometimes we know what happens to the person outwardly, but we do not know what is happening within the brain. Certain it is, though, that something wonderful happens sometimes when the angle and the motion or movement of the eyes are modified somewhat.

Now to the precise steps of techniques in learning how to read fast. But hold on to your hats: You are going to be doing some crazy things and in a short time, if you follow the directions given here, you are going to be reading swiftly. I promise!

Step One: Get a stopwatch or some other accurate timing device.

Step Two: Have on hand several story or reading books, nothing above third-grade level. Get the kind that have as few pictures as possible. Pictures will slow you down.

Step Three: Tell yourself that it is possible to read at tremenmendously fast speeds with good understanding. Remember, a person who reads faster enjoys more, learns more, and has more time for other things, including more reading.

Step Four: Have someone time you, and have that person say to you: "I am going to time you while you *look* at *all* the words on the first page of your book. You will have only five seconds to do this, so you must move your eyes very fast. But— you are not to try to understand the words. Remember, no comprehension! Ready, go!"

(After the first "timing" it will be necessary to discuss between you again the idea of "no comprehension." The above process is repeated many times, going from five seconds, to four seconds, to three seconds, etc.)

Step Five: "You are to see the words in any manner or direction in which you can see them best. The left-to-right pattern might be best for you, but it might not be, too. Some people can go faster and more comfortably by looking at the words straight down the page, or zigzagging, or going in spirals, or going down one page and up the next, or going down the left-hand page diagonally, and up the right-hand page diagonally, such as in a big V. You must try different patterns, with the book held at different angles."

I must reemphasize strongly the need for following the directions being given about experimenting and trying to find the best and most comfortable way of seeing the words on the page. Eye-movement pattern becomes extremely important. In doing this you are not only exercising your eye muscles, but you are also stimulating the brain in a way that is new to it, at least in reading.

Step Six: Three to four periods of thirty to sixty minutes should be devoted just to "seeing" words rapidly without trying to understand the meaning of them. The idea is to start from the beginning to get into the habit of seeing faster than most of us were taught to see in the reading process. (*Are you following directions?*)

Step Seven: Gradually move into comprehension. Have your helper say: "This time I want you to try to understand just two or three things about the story you are reading. [My wife has applied the term "un-reading" to this business of just seeing words rapidly without attempting to understand their meaning.] Be able to answer questions such as who, what, why, where, etc., but only two or three of them this time. *But do not slow down!* There is plenty of time for slowing down. You must continue to see the words as fast as you have been doing, maybe even faster. *And do not slow down!*"

(Remind yourself again and often about seeing the words at different angles, and experiment often with new eye-movement patterns.)

Step Eight: Your helper says, "Let's read again, this time try to pick up a little more information as you go. Do not slow down."

These directions should be repeated with variations, with more comprehension being added each time. As your comprehension improves, your helper should begin to ask you questions about what you see in your mind as you read. Do you see pictures? Do they have color? (Do you *dream* in color?) Do you "hear" *sounds* from the story you are reading? These are all important aspects of comprehension, but seldom, if ever, discussed in the reading classes in our schools.

I have found that emphasizing mental picturization is very helpful to many people. It is sometimes surprising the number of persons who do not have this kind of experience while reading. It actually enhances our reading pleasure and ability. If they do not already possess this ability, it behooves us to help them develop it. Many students tell us that they are better able to keep the sequence of the material better if the pictures have movement.

Some people appear to visualize only in black and white. I have found that often the more active the person, the more vivid and colorful his mental pictures will be. It is necessary to coach and encourage some people to attempt visualization in reading. I know a man who has a large, beautiful home. He can describe it because he built it and remembers the details, but he says he cannot see it in his "mind's eye." He cannot visualize the events he is reading about. It's sad. He is also lacking in some of the finer qualities which go to make up an empathetic person. He is unable to put himself, or see himself, in another person's place.

Step Nine: Continue these instructions, reemphasizing speed techniques, eye-movement patterns and comprehension development to yourself. You might have to slow down to gain better understanding. Certainly there is more than one speed at which you will want to read, depending on how you feel, the kind of material you are reading, your purpose in reading, etc. This is called "flexibility in reading." A good reader adapts his rate to his particular needs.

How fast are you reading in words per minute? You will want to test yourself many times along the way as you are practicing your reading. It helps to give impetus to your reading rate, and to motivate you to do better. The formula I use to quickly get my rate in wpm (words per minute) is as follows:

1. Count the number of words in the first ten lines of the material being read.
2. Divide that number by ten to get the average number of words per line.
3. Count *all* of the lines on a full page. Count the short lines and the long lines.
4. Multiply the average number of words per line by the number of words on a full page. This gives you the average number of words per page.)
5. Count the number of *full* pages. Beginnings and endings of chapters, pictures, etc., take up part of a page or all of the page. Put halves and thirds of pages together to make full pages.
6. Multiply the number of full pages you read by the number of words per page. If you have read for one minute, this will give you your rate per minute. If you read for two or more minutes you would, of course, divide by the latter number the total number of words you read.

Practice. You have to practice if you want to read better. It's just like anything else. If you want to learn something you have to work at it. For some of us, learning new things comes rather easily. Others have to work like mad to get what they want. I was one of those who had to spend a great deal of time in order to increase my speed very much. But then, I had no teacher, no class, and no instructions to follow. I was so enthusiastic about wanting to read faster that I went about it with much zeal and gusto. I even kept a book beside my bed and would wake up in the middle of the night and annoy my wife by turning on the light and practicing as I lay in bed. I kept an open book on my desk at school and would practice for a minute or two between classes.

I just had to learn how to read like a seventh-grader I had seen perform in rapid reading. She had read a book in a reading demonstration at the fantastic rate of eighteen hundred words a minute. I caught the bug. I figured if that seventh-grade kid could read that fast, then certainly I, a reading "expert," should be able to do it.

And I did, then began to use the idea in the reading clinic of which I was director. First I used it with the "smart" kids, then later with those who were having problems in reading. It worked. They loved it and wanted more of the same. Kids want to learn, you see. When we find one who doesn't, it's usually because he has been knocked down and stepped on several times during the learning process. That would discourage any of us.

But back to that practice business. You should devote at least thirty minutes a day to good, solid, concentrated practice; more if you can. Really throw yourself into it and practice on everything you can; things like road signs, advertisements, TV stuff, newspapers, and anything else that you don't have to read for good understanding. That is in the beginning. Later, as you work for good comprehension, use the same procedures but now you will be understanding more and more, until you finally achieve what we call "book report" comprehension.

In order to give you an idea on how you should be proceeding on a day-to-day basis, the following schedule should prove helpful. Remember, I promised you earlier that if you follow the instructions given herein you will become a faster reader. That was not an idle promise. However, if you do not follow the instructions, you have no promise. So proceed on the following basis:

Day One: Discuss the present methods of reading, brain development, angle of vision; think in terms of eye-movement patterns, eye-movement practice, and subvocalization and non-subvocalization.

Day Two: Review of yesterday, and enlarge on all items. Reading practice with emphasis on rate, and for some understanding—"bits and pieces" understanding. Remember angle of vision and eye movements. Turn pages *fast* when you are finished with them.

Day Three: Further emphasis on rate, and adding comprehension. Further check on brain development including cerebral dominance. That is, check to make sure you are either completely right-sided or left-sided. Make sure you begin performing all skills with your right side or left side, but not with *both* sides of the body. Check rate per minute. Add a little more comprehension. Get ready to increase your level of reading materials. Turn pages *fast*.

Day Four: Begin more emphasis on comprehension, but still with strong emphasis on rate. Use upper elementary level materials. New eye-movement experimentation and angle of vision. Reading rates in wpm.

Day Five: Strong emphasis on *comprehension;* decrease rate *if necessary*. Eye movement and positioning of material again. Get rate per minute often. Rapid page turning always.

Day Six: Develop new techniques of comprehension: Picturization, movement of visual pictures; color in pictures; sounds heard in reading. Increase level of reading materials as you can. Adjust rate, but increase speed if possible by starting each practice period with seeing words fast with no comprehension, then moving into comprehension.

Day Seven: Use of regular reading materials, i.e., use homework materials if a student, magazines, etc., materials used for everyday reading. Greater comprehension now. Don't forget mental pictures, etc. Rate per minute daily. Check on cerebral dominance.

Day Eight: Strong emphasis on comprehension continued, and push rate of reading, adjusting eye-movement pattern if necessary. Relate in detail what you read, giving time, sequence, etc. Reread for better comprehension if necessary.

Day Nine: Best comprehension with best or highest rate in wpm. All aspects of the above should be stressed. By this time you should have at least tripled your rate with good understanding if you have been faithful in following the instructions. Are you using the best eye-movement pattern for *you?* Go line by line if necessary, but go rapidly. You can if you practice as outlined, with your best pattern.

Before closing out this chapter I must tell you about Mary

Ann. She is a very unhappy second-grader. She taught herself to read when she was three years old, using her brother's first-grade books. Shortly after she became five, she was able to read very rapidly as a result of a special course she took in rapid reading. She read at high speeds from second-grade books at the time spoken of above. She has given more than a dozen demonstrations of her ability before public audiences in three states, has been on TV and radio many times, and was on a national radio show where she demonstrated her ability to read rapidly with understanding.

But Mary Ann is unhappy now in the second grade because her teacher insists that she must read from second-grade books because she is in second grade. These are books which she read two years ago. Last year when she was in the first grade, the principal of her school and her first-grade teacher required her to read from first-grade books. Finally, after many urgings from the parents, Mary Ann was permitted to read from a higher level reader, but was required to sit off by herself when she did so. She actually had to sit in the corner while her group read. The teacher told her parents that if she wanted to read something different from what the other children were reading, "She will just have to do it by herself." Mary Ann felt she was being punished for being a good reader, and so expressed herself that way to me.

As a result of all of this, Mary Ann had to be forced to go to school. Think of it! Punished for learning! Her parents literally had to spank her every morning for weeks to make her attend school. Morning after morning she played sick so she would not have to go. Being a child and being realistic and honest, she said she was not learning anything, so why go to school? She had a good point, did she not? But it didn't change anything; she still had to go to school. She decided she did not want to be off by herself while the other children read, and finally told the teacher that she would like to read what they were reading. The teacher made the comment to the parents that she was "glad that Mary Ann had finally come to her senses and is reading like the other children." Even now as I write this it makes my blood boil to remember the stupidity of some (not all) teachers, and some administrators.

Today Mary Ann is still very unhappy in school, but she says that it is a little better now because she has found a "boy-friend" who helps her pass the time. (Thank goodness for boy-friends!) Her teacher recently told Mary Ann's mother that the second-grade books would be good for the child, and when the mother told her that Mary Ann had read those books a long time ago, the teacher replied: "You should not have allowed her to do that." (At this point I want to use a lot of swear words and don't quite know how without actually putting them in print.) So after a year and a half of frustration and confusion on her part, Mary Ann lost interest in school and says she wants to be a dropout.

So I say again: Damn the school system—full speed ahead! And I want to say it still again as I recall that my daughter's teacher told her one day that she did not think I should have taught her how to read rapidly. "Because," she said, "it makes too much work for the teacher." But it was when that daughter was in the sixth grade and I was trying to get the teacher to let her read other books because she had read most of those in the room—it was then that I finally broke down and cursed at that teacher. The teacher had just said: "Well, if she *has* to read something else, she can read the encyclopedia." That was when I swore at her.

Chapter III

How to Get Paid
For Teaching Children
Without Teaching Children

Guess what! Wonders will never cease. Last night my fourth-grade daughter brought home her reader! Sure enough she did. I asked her how come? It was a natural question. This was the first time in five years of school (she went to kindergarten) that she had been allowed to do this. As I have pointed out before, the reading textbook is almost Holy Writ and, like the Bible of old that was chained to the pulpit, this book is almost chained to the schoolroom. The child is seldom allowed to take it home.

But there it was, big as life and twice as pretty. So I asked why. My daughter told me that if she hadn't brought it home she would have had to stay after school to do some work in it. "What kind of work?" I asked. "Yuk," she answered. It seems that during reading class that day she was supposed to have written down a list of words from the book, then broken the words into syllables. Instead, she had read, sneakily, the next story in the book, and now was taking the consequences. She had to do it at home or else get an F, so the teacher told her to take home the book and do the work, but cautioned her not to do any reading in it other than that particular assignment.

I asked her if she enjoyed doing that kind of assignment, and again received the enlightening "Yuk." "I hate it," she said. "Why can't they let us read the book instead of having to write so much of it?" My heart went out to her, but being a dutiful parent and a supporter of my children's teachers, I encouraged the girl to go ahead and do her assignment. I didn't want her to get an F, you see.

The schools make a big deal of American Education Week

in November. It's at this time that there is much ballyhoo about all good parents visiting the schools and seeing what their children are doing, and how fine the schools are. It is a good idea for the parents to do this. We need to see what things are like there, but not during American Education Week. The teachers are really prepared for us then, and the rooms are beautifully arranged and the kids are warned to be on their best behavior.

Wait a minute, now. Before you start saying that that just isn't so, let me tell you that I'll bet I have visited more classrooms than *you* have, and I know what goes on. Oh, I don't mean that *every* teacher puts on that kind of front, but you can bet your life that most of them (us) want to make a good impression on the parents when they come to visit. Heck, I don't blame them: It just makes good sense. What I'm saying is that we don't usually get invited except during Education Week, and that's not when I want to visit, but I don't receive an invitation except during that one week. Just let me walk into that school any other time and you can't count the dirty looks I get.

But let me tell you what happened one day during Education Week when I accepted the invitation of the school and visited my kids' classrooms. I stayed longer in each of their rooms than most of the other parents because I wanted to see the kids in action in a number of situations. (I left when I saw the teachers were getting nervous.) What I saw made me both angry and frustrated because I was helpless to do anything about it.

I observed social studies, math, and reading being "taught." With the exception of math, the teaching was the same as that of a hundred years ago. I mean most of the methods were the same ones I had been taught thirty years ago while I was in a teacher training institute, and about the same as when I was in the elementary schools as a pupil.

To illustrate: In one class I visited the children were studying Scotland in social studies. They were taking turns reading parts of the assignment aloud, each one taking a turn as he was called on by the teacher. It was not an "up and down the row" thing, I noticed, and when the opportunity presented itself, I asked the teacher about it. She told me that she felt that the lesson had to be read aloud in order that those youngsters who were poor readers could get some of the information. They could not read silently themselves, she said. That's true, of course. The social studies books in the elementary schools are the most difficult to read because of the type of vocabulary they have.

So what the teacher was saying and doing made some sense— in a way. But we know that what we do not understand we do not learn well. Those kids who did not read well were not allowed to read orally from the material that day. Naturally, the teacher wanted to make a good impression on the parents and wanted things to go smoothly. Who can blame her? But in conversation with her she whispered: "But you know, and I know, that those kids aren't going to get it anyway, no matter what I do."

So why was she having the lesson presented that way? Why not change the procedure? I even had the temerity to suggest, very gently of course, that perhaps not all of the children had to learn about the amount of rain that usually falls in Scotland, and what it does or does not to the industrial growth of that country. "Perhaps," I said, "some of the kids could be making a war map of Israel and Egypt, since there was much trouble brewing over there." But the teacher assured me she could not possibly have the youngsters divided that way, because after all they were all in the same grade and they had to progress in an orderly way through the textbook.

Then she smiled at me in a rather superior way and almost triumphantly said: "I know something about your way of thinking and some of the radical ideas you have. [I wonder where she learned them; I had never had her in a class.] But here we like to have all of the children move along together from grade to grade, and that means that we must complete the textbook so that the next teacher can take up where I leave off."

You see, there we go again. "Move along together." There just seems to be no place for the child who is more capable; the child who is bored stiff with school except for recess and gym. Every child, it seems, must learn the same thing at the same time, or he fails. Once I asked a fifth-grade teacher what would happen if a pupil failed to pass a test this year on the events surrounding the American Revolution. He replied that the pupil would fail if he were in *his* class. "But," I said, "suppose he learns it well next year, what then? Will he be any less a good citizen if he doesn't learn it today but learns it tomorrow? Or next year?"

Don't get me wrong. I believe there are some things that we should all learn in order for us to be better citizens, but as to exactly when we should learn some of these things is what bothers me, and the emphasis we place on them in the schoolroom at certain times. For example, there is the story of the boy in the sixth grade who had to repeat that grade because he just could not learn well. Among other things, he was supposed to learn the names of the presidents of the United States. He couldn't seem to remember their names in the right order and had to stay after school often in order to complete that particular assignment. He spent the next year in the same grade, but this time had a different teacher. By then he had forgotten most of the names of the presidents, except for a few of the well-known ones, but it didn't matter so much now because his new teacher was not so interested in the names of the presidents. He felt the children should learn the names of the great inventors in America.

Do you see what I mean? Our values differ, and the emphasis we place on some things today will be different tomorrow. And in school this means that the children are exposed to, and become the victims of, the whims of the teachers. Perhaps the names of the presidents and the names of the great American inventors are all of vital importance, but are they of the same importance at a given time?

Back to the point of my disagreement with the teacher who was having the children (some of the best readers) read aloud the part concerning the amount of rainfall in Scotland. Was this of such importance to all the kids that none of them should have been engaged in other more meaningful activities? The teacher seemed to think so since she was having them do it. But her whispered confidence to me that some of the kids would never get it no matter what she did demonstrates the falseness of her actions, and believe you me, this is *not* an isolated situation. I have encountered it many times in every subject matter area. It doesn't matter whether it is high school math or first-grade reading. The same kind of thinking too often prevails: Every pupil is expected to do the same thing at the same time, and get the same results.

Later, when the teacher was to give a test on this assignment, she would give the same test to all the pupils. She would hope, of course, that all the kids would respond with A's, but it would naturally be a false hope. She already knows which ones will fail or not do well enough to make more than a low average grade. She even told me in advance that this would happen.

I remember only too well visiting a student teacher in the accounting class he was teaching. He told me that he already knew five students who would fail the course. This was in September, mind you. Instead of agreeing with him, I startled him by asking him if he expected every student to do the same kind of work and produce the same kind of results. He didn't know what to say, but the answer was obvious. I asked him then what he was going to do about it. He hadn't even thought about it, apparently, and neither had his supervising teacher, after whom the student teacher was patterning his teaching.

Continuing the story of my visit to my children's classrooms, I observed a fifth-grade reading class in operation. Here again the children took turns reading, with the "good" readers getting to read at longer lengths than the "poor" ones. There was some discussion of the material being read, then the pupils were told to get out their workbooks and do pages 44-47. This meant that they would answer some questions, write lists of words that looked alike or sounded alike, compare certain words listed at the top of the page, etc. Some of the kids finished their work rapidly; others didn't finish at all, but it kept them busy, and that was supposed to look good to the parents who were visiting. I got bored and left, much to the pleasure of the teacher. She was quite nervous all the time I was there, and kept looking at me to see whether or not I approved of what she was doing. I didn't, but decided not to tell her I didn't. I was trying to act like a parent who was visiting his child's classroom, but it was difficult, and it was difficult to keep quiet as I saw my child not learning anything he didn't already know. He is a good reader, and a fast one, and if they would let him alone, he would read everything they had that interested him; things like sports, science, etc. But when they had him draw lines under words, and write down lists of words that sounded alike, etc., he got bored and started making mistakes.

Isn't that something? This boy is an excellent reader, with a vocabulary far above that of the grade level he is in, but he gets B's and C's in language arts because of the tripe they insist on giving him. Recently when he told me that he hates language arts I grieved for him. That poor kid: he reminded me all the world of that selection called "The Animal School," by G. H. Reavis. In that story the ducks, squirrels, eagles, and rabbits all had to take the same courses, because that way the curriculum was easier to administer.

The duck was among the slowest in the running class, so he had to stay after school to do makeup work, and as a result his web feet became so sore that he became only average in swimming. The rabbit, on the other hand, began at the top of the class in running, but had to do so much makeup work in swimming that he had a nervous breakdown and had to quit school. The squirrel was excellent in climbing, but became completely frustrated in the flying class because the teacher made him start at the bottom and go up. He finally developed "charley horses" from overexertion, then got a C in climbing and D in running. The eagle drove the teacher crazy because in the climbing class he could beat all the others to the top of a tree, but insisted on his own way of getting there. He was punished for not following the rules.

And so my son is developing a dislike for language arts because he must do a lot of stuff that he already knows how to do, and is bored and hates the teacher; so he says. I don't blame him, but I can't tell him that I agree with him, because I am supposed to support the teacher in his stupidity. Guess that makes me stupid too. Blast it!

On my visit to my kids' classrooms during Education Week, I also watched a math class in progress. Now, with this "new" math, or "modern" math, great things are supposed to happen. Maybe they are; maybe it was an "off day" on the particular day I visited, but likely not. I've had occasion to watch hundreds of math classes in session, and this was not an exception. Oh, the kids were doing their problems differently from the way you and I learned them, and even different from the way I used to teach math, but again, every child was doing the same assignment, had the same amount of time in which to do it, and was given the same test. What we often call the "basics" in math were being taught exactly the same way I was taught them forty-six years ago, and the way I was taught to teach them more than thirty years ago. As a college student remarked only this morning, "We are programmed to do certain things in certain ways, and good or bad, that's the way we do them."

In this math class it was evident that some of the kids were really going to town, while others were having to labor, and some fell by the way. Those who finished their work first were rewarded by being allowed to color turkeys, because they were getting ready for Thanksgiving already. All of the children had the same problems to do, and of course, were using the same books. You see, in math, which is a highly sacred subject, there are no gradations in the books such as there are in the reading textbooks. In the latter area we have as many as three or four levels in use in one room. Not so in math. If a first-grader can't do math, then we say he simply is not ready for first grade. The same thing is said of him in reading, but at least we have three sets of readers with which to work with him.

A little later I want to tell you of some exciting things being done in math and spelling, but right now let me expand on this business of a child being too "immature" to enter first grade. When this happens we just keep him another year in kindergarten. That'll do the trick nearly every time. And anyway, you just cannot keep a child *three* years in kindergarten, can you?

So we *make* him be ready for the first grade after two years in kindergarten.

You parents whose children have been the victims, or near victims, of this heinous practice, was it ever suggested by anyone that instead of requiring the child to adapt to the first grade that perhaps the first grade should adapt to him? I'll bet it wasn't. Yet it can be done, and if the school is to do what it purports to do, this adaptation must take place. Children can be taught reading and math at very early ages; earlier than first grade and kindergarten. This we know; this we have done. It is not theory; it is a fact, but it is the way that we teach the children that automatically makes them "too immature" for first grade. All we have to do is to change our philosophy and our methods, and every child who is anywhere near normal or average can make the grade. I know: I have done it.

As I said before, my three youngest children learned to read before they started kindergarten. I even had my own preschool reading program in which there were youngsters from three to five years old. They all learned to read quickly. And you remember Mary Ann who taught herself to read at the age of three. I get awfully tired of hearing teachers say that this child, or that child, is not ready to start first grade because of his immaturity: That's a lot of hogwash. It's the teacher who doesn't know how to adapt her teaching to the needs of the individual. I believe that she should be told to either do the job or get out.

We do some crazy, odd, and stupid things in the name of education. The other day I came out of a school building feeling discouraged and almost sick. I was deciding again that I had better quit the teaching profession. It just seemed as though there was no progress being made despite what I had been trying to do.

I had just spent an hour observing a student teacher at work in a special education class, then had talked with her for a half hour out in the corridor. She told me that what I had seen in her room was the usual kind of thing that went on there. Now, this was in a hotshot school system which prided itself on its fine educational practices. Indeed, I *know* it is a good school system. How do I know, you ask. I know because the superin-

tendent of schools there told me so himself. See? Now, if what
I'm going to tell you is indicative of a *good* school system, just
think what it must be to have a child in one that is *not* that good.
And if you should have a child in special education in that
system, then watch out below!

The chalk board was full of announcements and assignments.
The youngsters in that room devoted the entire day to writing
and reading in their workbooks and textbooks. There was absolutely no equipment of any kind except for a map and a globe.
As a pupil completed one page or sheet of his assignment, he
was told to do the next part, or to go to the table where a group
was taking turns reading from a reading textbook. That story
was repeated again and again as new kids came to the table.
When they left the table it was to go back to their desks and
their workbooks where they would do the assignment that went
along with the textbooks. When they finished that, they would
do social studies, again using that ever-present workbook. And
so it went all day, the student teacher told me.

I had talked with the young teacher previously in my office
about her situation, and suggested that perhaps she would like
to be placed in a different school. But she had said that these
kids really needed someone with some fresh ideas, and that maybe
she would have the opportunity to present some sometime. So
she stayed and eventually was able to do a few things. Not many,
you understand, but a few. The supervising teacher told her
that she (the supervisor) had been teaching in that very room
for ten years, and that she found it quite stimulating, and that
she liked the room the way it was. And that's the way it still is!
Evidently it will stay that way too, because the superintendent
thinks his school system is one of the best.

In this particular classroom in this "good" school system,
few if any of the advantages that the mentally retarded should
have are available. There is no special equipment, the room is too
small to accommodate very much anyway, and there was absolutely no provision made for individual differences. The kids
were all using copies of the same books and the same workbooks,
and identical, especially prepared worksheets were passed to each

child as the time came for that particular lesson. It was a dull, deadly classroom, and I came away from there terribly discouraged. I went home and told my wife that I had decided to quit trying to change things. Why not just teach the same old way that so many of the teachers seem to like, and not try to make waves? My wife upbraided me severely and reminded me that I was not yet as Job. She pointed out that there are some places where real progress is being made, and that I should be ashamed of myself for even thinking of becoming a quitter. She called me a dropout. That hurt, so I didn't drop out.

It is true that there are many good, even great, teachers around. These, she said, we must put our hope in, and trust that eventually many more will decide that teaching children means just that. This particular special education room in which I was observing that day was, hopefully, not indicative of all such rooms. I have seen other classrooms where the mentally retarded are really treated like human beings, where human dignity is upheld and sought after. But the thing that frightened me and discouraged me was the thought that there must be thousands of classrooms across the country where this type of teaching obtains. As I think about it now it makes me more sad than mad, I guess. I feel like crying.

But I suppose that special education room was no worse than another classroom I visited one day. It was a "regular" fourth-grade room with about twenty-eight pupils. On this occasion the class was engaged in studying social studies, and all of the youngsters were supposed to be working on their social studies notebooks. But one boy in particular seemed to be having trouble. He kept getting out of his desk without permission from either the supervising teacher or the student teacher, and this simply was not allowed. I guess they had been having some difficulty before I arrived, and they didn't know what else to do. Anyway, after speaking again to him in a loud voice, the supervising teacher stepped over to him and aimed a kick at the boy. He dodged the teacher, who nearly fell over as she became unbalanced. I almost burst trying to keep from laughing. Of course, the teacher became enraged, grabbed the boy, slapped his face, and marched him back to his seat.

Order was restored. The teacher explained to me: "That big dumb ox! One of these days he's going to learn that he can't fool around in here." She went on to say that this boy was a constant troublemaker and consistently refused to do his work. It seems that one of the things he would not, or could not, do was his social studies, and this was a focal point as far as that teacher was concerned. Apparently she was determined that he was going to do it, and he was just as determined not to. She took measures: "He has not seen the light of day at recess in six weeks," she triumphantly declared. She had been making him stay in at recess until he brought his social studies notebook up to date, and he certainly stayed in on this particular day!

There was another situation in that room which interested me. There was a rule that no one could speak or get out of his seat without permission from the teacher. As I watched the class one day I noticed a girl suddenly raise her hand in the air. She waited expectantly to be recognized by the supervising teacher or by the student teacher, but neither one of them paid her any attention. After a bit her arm became tired, I suppose, so the girl propped the raised arm with the other, and the upraised arm continued upraised.

I am not exaggerating one iota when I tell you that this situation continued for five minutes. Finally the student teacher "recognized" the girl and asked her what she wanted. The girl said: "I broke the lead of my pencil. May I go to the pencil sharpener?" Permission was given.

When I realized what had happened I became incensed and could hardly wait to get that student teacher aside so I could kick her britches, but it turned out that it wasn't her idea to have such a rule. It had been made before she got there and she had to help enforce it.

I don't even like to think of the number of possible times that stupidity of that kind has kept children from learning. Is that teacher still in the classroom? How many years did a school principal let that happen? But the dreadful thing about it is that it *is* going on right now. A few days ago one of my student teachers in a first-grade setting allowed some kids to go to a pencil sharpener, and three of them congregated there at once. There was no confusion: they were speaking quietly to one another as they sharpened their pencils.

Suddenly a thunderbolt descended upon them in the form of the supervising teacher. "You know you are not supposed to sharpen your pencils except after recess. Who gave you permission to do it now?" The children didn't know quite what to say, but the student teacher bravely spoke up and confessed that she was the culprit. She hadn't realized that such a rule was in effect. The supervising teacher gave her a hard look, and then sent the kids skedaddling back to their seats. She explained to the young teacher that she just could not stand confusion and wanted everything done "in orderly fashion." Again, no child was allowed out of his desk without permission, and could sharpen his pencil only immediately after recess. If we don't put down learning one way, we'll certainly do it another. We'll make them all just alike or know the reason why.

I want to pursue that thought further. This same first-grade teacher was a well-organized person and had things just as she wanted them in her classroom. She even told the student teacher once that "I guess I'm just old-fashioned, but I've been doing this [she was speaking of an artificial fireplace that she put in her room every Christmas season] for ten years in this very room, and I find it works very well." She wasn't old-fashioned: She was stupid and ignorant. Stupid, she was because she would not see anything else, and ignorant because she didn't know how to look for something new.

The student teacher, who was highly skilled in art, had asked her boss if she could do some rearranging of the room for Christmastime and put up some new things with the help of the teacher. "No," said this "old-fashioned" teacher, "I like it this way." And remember what I said many pages back about that first-grade teacher who had outlasted several principals because she obeyed the rules? (Now wait a minute! I'm not suggesting that we go about breaking rules just because we don't like something, but I am suggesting that we remove the chains of bondage from the minds of young people and let them do things that have been impossible, but are no longer that way.) That first-grade teacher who obeyed the rules so well kept her job, and the poor kids perhaps never knew that they missed much more learning and fun.

Remember what Jean Piaget, the Swiss psychologist, said about what our schools are supposed to be doing: "The principal goal of education," he said, "is to create men (and women) who are capable of doing *new things*, not simply of repeating what other generations have done—men who are creative, inventive, and discoverers."

Then remember those kids who cannot speak without permission in the classroom, who can't go to the pencil sharpener without the good word from the teacher, who line up to go to the rest room at a given time, who follow carefully the assignments given in the workbook, and do just so much and no more. Remember the kids who can't read more than one story a day and are punished if they dare read two, and the kids who must all do the same pages in the math book even if they already know how to do those problems. Remember, too, those youngsters who get fifteen spelling words a week and must define each one, write a sentence using each one of the words, then break up each word into syllables—all of this when many of the kids already know how to spell the cockeyed words. Is it any wonder that the schoolrooms have been called grim and joyless places? Is it any wonder that one of the head men working on behalf of the disadvantaged said that every child who enters school becomes disadvantaged?

Is it any wonder that one mother wrote from San Francisco saying, "Won't you please help me? Sally was bored last year in kindergarten because all they did was color things and play games. Now in the first grade she is bored still because she has to do the things that every other child does when she already knows how to do them well. She wants to quit school. A first-grade dropout. And to think I have to pay taxes for this stuff they insist on giving her. *Please, help me!*"

It is a damnable thing. What can parents do? If they go to the school and ask that their child be given something more challenging they are termed troublemakers. "Oh, oh, here comes

Mrs. Smith again. I wonder what she wants *this* time?" And the particular Mrs. Smith who wrote me the foregoing letter had been told by the principal of the school, "Just don't you worry. We're taking care of Sally." He went on to tell her that she was too worried about the girl and that if she just wouldn't come around quite so much Sally would be better off. "Sure," said the mother, "if I don't come around, Sally will keep right on doing what she is now—wanting to quit school!" And then she added in her letter: "Oh, how I would like to kick that principal right in the seat of his learning!"

Damn the school system—Full speed ahead—y'all.

Chapter IV

The Case of the Puttering Principal

Then there is the "Case of the Puttering Principal." A while back I asked a young teacher who was complaining about his school, just what he would want to do to change it. "Well, first of all," he said, "I would get rid of the principal."

"Why, what's the matter with the principal," I asked. (The principal had told me that he [himself] was a good schoolman; one who knows his business.)

"He putters," came the answer from the new teacher. So I asked just exactly what that meant, and got a reply that made me realize again what blasted fools we are as parents and educators. That is, we *let* this kind of thing happen again and again.

The principal runs a tight ship. No one is allowed to walk down the middle of the hallway. He must keep to one side of the hall. Even in their military-like lines to and from the bathrooms, the children have to keep one shoulder against the wall. And on such occasions they are to walk tippy-toe so as not to disturb other classes. Now, I happen to know from personal experience that this young teacher was not exaggerating in this respect. I was in that building one day when a fifth-grade teacher decided that it was bathroom time. (It's just pure uncanniness the way the elementary teacher decides that every child has to use the bathroom at a certain time. Do you suppose the teacher himself . . . ?) The kids lined up at the door to get ready to go out. That is, all but two of them. They had had a little contest to see who was going to head the line (no pun intended!), and both lost. The teacher made them wait until all the others were out the door, then they were allowed to bring up the end of the line.

The girls went first. Ladies always go first there, the teacher told me, even to the bathroom. The teacher stood just outside the room doorway and whispered to each child to keep his left shoulder against the wall, and to follow the leader. The leader was going tippy-toe. Tight ship!

It was a clean ship, too. I didn't see any of Grandma's lye soap around, but there were some mighty clean floors in that building. I'll tell you why. From the time of the first snow until snow time is over, no child plays outside the building. The kids clean their shoes thoroughly before they are allowed in the building. And listen to this: The janitress is the one who really enforces the rule which the principal has laid down. And the teachers seem to cower before her. They are all one big happy family in that school, you see, what with the principal of the school being the brother-in-law of the janitress' husband, and with the janitress being the cousin of one of the teachers.

There are no innovations in that school, I'll tell you. The principal told me confidentially one day that one of the members of the institution where I teach had tried one time to conduct some experimental programs in his school. "But," the principal told me, "we kind of like to think that we have the kind of school here that the parents like. And when you have satisfied parents," he said, "you have nothing to worry about." Maybe he is right. The mother who wrote that letter to me was certainly not satisfied and was giving her principal something to worry about.

My "Puttering Principal" (I wonder how many there are of this kind in our schools) works hard. I've seen him many times sitting in the teachers' lounge with his cup of coffee. Indeed, I've seldom seen him in his office. Now, one can be out of his office and doing a right good job as principal, but this one was not around in the rooms nor the halls. He was in the teachers' lounge. He always jumped up and greeted me enthusiastically, would invite me to have a cup of coffee, and when I refused, he would take me out into the hallway and show me how nice things looked.

He also showed me the library, which was bright and uncluttered; not a book on the tables; not one. It was a clean room.

The rug on the floor had been there two years, he told me, and it looked almost as good as new. Each grade in the school was allowed in the library for thirty minutes once a week, "as long as they do not misuse it," he told me. I was afraid to ask him what he meant by that for fear of what I would hear, but the stern look that came over his face assured me that dreadful things must happen when it is "misused." Again the same old story: Each child is allowed to check out one book a week, and may keep it just one week. If he wishes to keep it two weeks he must re-sign for it. Tight ship.

How am I going to tell you about this next part without bursting out laughing again? I know—I'll think about how darned dumb and stupid the whole thing was, utterly stupid! Even as I think about it now, I wonder about the sanity of human beings who are supposed to be educating our children. Truly, it's a damnable situation.

We again find the "Puttering Principal," this time in a different location. He had called a special faculty meeting for after school and none of the teachers could figure out why. Three forty-five arrived and the teachers assembled. The janitor was there, also, carrying a paper bag. The principal opened the meeting, then told the faculty that the janitor had something to show us. The mystery of the paper bag was solved! It was full of wads of gum stuck together. In solemn but angered tones, the janitor related how he had been going around tipping over desks and removing the wads of gum stuck thereunder. This was his collection. He gave a short (he was a man of few words) but eloquent speech on how the underside of the desks had been disfigured with the unsightly stuff, and how much work it had been to clean it off. He also said one or two words about the teachers and children who chew gum.

The principal then gave an eloquent speech also. In stern tones he commanded the teachers "to bend every effort to stamp out this ugly practice of chewing gum in school. We absolutely will not tolerate it." He then asked the teachers to "send to my office any child who persists in chewing gum in class, or even on the playground." The janitor had previously commented on the unsightly gum wrappers on the playgrounds. He was a real ecologist, I guess. He didn't like bending over either; he had a bad back.

All during the meeting the teachers "neither smiled nor laughed, but said right down, 'I will.' " They became imbued with the ideals of the Great Crusade—to stamp out gum chewing. As the meeting was breaking up, one of the teachers whispered to another: "Do you suppose Bill (the janitor) was looking for a *clean* wad of gum for himself under those desks?" Shame on that teacher!

But there the story does *not* end. The grabbing of the gum began. One of the teachers, a new one, apparently wanting to make a good name for himself, was especially ardent in his efforts to eradicate the awful practice. After warning his pupils and re-warning them as to the dangers that would come from it, he found one sixth-grade girl chomping away—and she actually seemed to be enjoying it! Unthinkable! But the teacher took steps! He made that girl take out all the rest of the sticks of gum she had, come to the front of the room, and stand there and chew all five sticks at the same time! He'd show her!

Well, he did. The girl stood there and chewed and laughed and giggled, and the whole class enjoyed it thoroughly. Then suddenly the girl toppled over. She had fainted. Maybe it was the excitement and the standing too long in one place, and the onset of young maturity. Anyway, there she went. It scared the young teacher to death almost. He sent a child for the principal, but by the time that worthy had arrived the girl was sitting up grinning feebly and somewhat embarrassedly, but still chomping away on the gum!

That was the last time that teacher would have anything more to say about gum chewing in school. Against the evils of it, any-way. He even began going the other direction. He (after some discussion with a former professor) did a bit of research, but came up with nothing really tangible. You see, he could not even find *one piece* of research pertaining to gum chewing and its effects on learning. Perhaps there has been some done, but he couldn't find it, and neither can I. Let me point out that there have been research studies made on nearly everything that pertains to school life, everything from the number of times a kid goes to the rest room to the number of cavities per tooth per kid. *But few if any on the effects of gum chewing on learning.* Do you suppose this is because there aren't any bad effects?

Teachers often make a big deal of this gum business, but have you noticed that they are the only ones who do? They and the principal, that is. A person can go into any public place in the country and chew to his heart's content, but let him step inside a school building and—*Pow!* Right *out* of the kisser!

I've just got to tell you this one, too, but you'd better hold onto your sides as I tell it.

It was Christmastime and the school was putting on a big program to be given at night. It would involve many of the kids in the school. The principal was in charge of it because, as he told me during the preparation of it, "I want this to be *really* good." I learned later that he had issued special invitations to the members of the school board to attend the performance.

The preparations were big and time-consuming. Classes were dismissed at any time for rehearsals, etc. Now, the principal was a realistic sort of person. Perhaps he could even be called a realist. He wanted to have real animals for the manger scene. (This was in the days before a bunch of smart people got wise to the fact that we had been teaching Christianity in the schools too long.) But finally saner thought prevailed, and the principal settled for something less. But he did want a donkey, and since it did not seem advisable to bring one onto the stage at the given time, donkeys being difficult to housebreak on short notice, he decided on another course of action. He would bring a donkey onto the tennis court where it would cast a neat and smooth shadow, place a large cardboard on the court right in the way of the shadow, and draw around the shadow. Then he would cut around the outline and—presto! The exact shape and size of a donkey!

You say, why didn't he have one of the artists in the school draw a donkey? Heck, I don't know. He said he wanted it to be a *good* program. And he was a realist, remember. Well, semi-, anyway.

He got a donkey (there were a lot of them around) and the desired cardboard, and placed both in the right position on the tennis court. He had had to wait for the sun to shine too, at just the right angle. You see, the tennis court was so situated that the backstop consisted of one side of the auditorium with a classroom or two as a sidestop. And thereby hangs (hung) a tale! All was in readiness for the big drawing. The donkey was sleepy and relaxed, just as it was hoped he would be, and an especially chosen teacher for the occasion was holding the rope at the donkey's neck. The principal was doing the drawing (he could trust no one else to do a good job), absorbed with his work, and slowly moving around the donkey with his drawing pencil.

He had just reached a point at the back of the donkey when the animal moved a bit, and the principal shouted to the teacher to "Hold him still!" Well, the teacher tried, but doggone it! *Someone* had forgotten to take the donkey to the bathroom before the drawing began, and the donkey, undoubtedly mistaking the tennis court for the bathroom——!

That's right, and right on the principal who was in the direct line of fire. The principal reacted with righteous indignation thinking perhaps that the donkey had done it deliberately. He slammed a kick at the donkey's belly and the donkey slammed one back. The donkey missed but the drawing ended. It had almost been completed anyway and the principal decided that he could finish it without the help of *any* jackass.

I would be lying if I were to say that the story ended there. Let me refer again to the position of the tennis court in relation to the auditorium and one wing of classrooms. It was an L-shaped affair, with the tennis court fitting into the L. The day of the drawing was a warm day, apparently, with a soft breeze blowing. Both the auditorium, which was very much in use at that time, and the classrooms wing of the building were downwind from the tennis court, and the odors wafted in on the breeze were not those of sweet-smelling roses. The drawing, incidentally, and the events appertaining thereto, had been witnessed by more than a few students and teachers. One could even say truthfully that the donkey had been cheered on in its efforts. The audience, it appears, would have been willing even to help bury Caesar.

So the odors from the tennis court brought forth many cries of distress, and soon the janitor was dispatched with broom, shovel, and bucket to clean up the tennis court. But, as was learned later by members of the faculty, he did so under duress. It seems that he had warned the principal before the event and now, in a loud voice, said, "I told you so." He did not feel that under the circumstances it was his place to clean up the mess. But he did—and quit his job that night. The word went around that he and the principal had had a big war of words, and the janitor quit. The Christmas program, subsequently, was a big success, but the principal was fired shortly after Christmas and the janitor rehired. The janitor, you see, had friends in high places. And not a jackass in the crowd!

The Red Cross drive was on and the principal had sent the necessary materials to each teacher along with a note saying, "Let's go over the top" in this particular matter. All but two of the teachers responded nobly. These two did not respond at all. Subsequently, they each received a letter from the principal saying that inasmuch as *you* did not give, she was asking those who *did* give to give again to make up for the dereliction of duty on their part. The teachers asked for an appointment with the principal and got it. They were met with stern cold eyes. Before they had a chance to speak, the principal berated them for their lack of patriotism, their lack of humanity, and their selfishness. Selfish, not only because they did not give, but also because they were letting other teachers give in their place.

Finally the teachers were allowed to speak, and pointed out that this was a matter of volunteer giving, not a requirement. To which the principal responded by saying that the school district was paying their salary and that the board of education was behind this drive, and they had better watch their step.

Such talk as this, of course, did not go over in a big way. However, one of the teachers, apparently beginning to see the light, took out her checkbook and, with an apology, wrote a check and left the office, confident that her job was secure. The other teacher asked the principal if he could use her telephone. She asked whom he wanted to call. He said the newspaper office. She asked why. He said he thought someone there would be interested in what she had to say about giving to the Red Cross or be threatened with losing some jobs.

Ahem! After some further discussion, it was agreed that the whole matter should be dropped. However the teacher still has in his possession the letter which the principal wrote telling him how awful he had been for not giving, and thereby making others give more. Blackmail? But he said he just wants "to keep it as a memento."

The other day I was visiting in that school and went into the teachers' lounge to wait for a student teacher whom I wanted to see. A young fellow was sitting there by himself and we greeted each other somewhat effusively. He was a former student of mine and I had gotten to know him fairly well a couple of years before. He said he was really seething. I asked why. This is what he told me.

He had been walking up the stairs when, on an impulse, he decided to hurry. He did so by running up the last half dozen steps, taking two at a time. At the top he came face to face with the principal, who reminded him that running on the steps was against the rules, "even for teachers," she said. "It sets a bad example for the children," she went on to say. She also told him that it was undignified for a man in his position to run on the stairs, and what would the children have thought of him had they seen him. "You must maintain your dignity and your position as a teacher at all times," she told him.

He asked me what I thought of that old so-and-so. I told him I didn't think of her at all unless I had to, but that he should abide by the rules of the school. That time I was sure enough lying, but what else could I do? We have to keep student teachers in that school. But I did tell him to check his surroundings the next time he decides to practice his running on the stairs.

Chapter V

How to Keep Kids From Learning Math and Spelling

I was sitting on my front porch one noon hour when one of our neighborhood kids hurried by. I called to him: "Bill, what's your hurry?" He stopped to reply, "I've got to get back and study my spelling words. We're having a test today and I've got to write the words I missed yesterday. I've got to write each word forty times before one o'clock." So I told him he'd better hurry on, but did think to ask him how many he had missed. "Ten," he replied, and he ran on.

Forty times ten, I thought, would equal four hundred. He had to write four hundred spelling words after lunch and before one o'clock. Good luck, I thought. You'll need it.

I saw Billy the next day after school and asked him how he did on the spelling test. "I missed twelve," he said. There had been nineteen words on the test, as it turned out, and after writing forty times each the words he had missed the day before, and now having taken a test on the same words that he had taken the day before, he had missed twelve. I didn't ask him if ten of the twelve were the same ones he had missed the day before. He didn't seem too interested in talking about it. He said he had to write each of the twelve words ten times, but that he had the whole weekend in which to do it. I gathered that Sunday night would be soon enough for him to think about them again. Poor kid.

Some lousy teacher, not being very smart, could not understand that making that kid write each word ten or forty times each was not helping him. Maybe she wanted to teach him discipline. She surely wasn't teaching him to spell, or even want to. Bill, incidentally, failed his grade that year and had to repeat it.

However, the good Lord had not forgotten him entirely, and he was placed under a different teacher the following September.

Bill's father went to see the principal one day to see if Bill could be given some special attention. He was doing poorly in all of his subjects. Some heat developed during the discussion, with the principal threatening to place Bill in the Special Education class, "if you're not careful," the principal said to Bill's father. It seems that Bill had been given an I.Q. test and had scored below 78 on it; therefore he was qualified to be placed in that class. It was a real threat, indeed, because everyone knew that once there, one stayed and was marked forever.

Later it was found that the test Bill had taken was one of those which required a great deal of reading, and since Bill was a poor reader, naturally he scored low. His father asked me to test Bill using some other kind of test. I administered the Wechsler Intelligence Scale for Children (WISC) and he scored an overall of 118. A fit subject for Special Education? And that principal and teacher were getting paid for treating that Bill, and who knows how many more Bills, as though he were less than human.

I went into a third-grade classroom one day just as they were getting ready for their spelling test. The nice teacher gave me a book from which the test was to be administered, and pointed out the page of words they would be using. There were eleven words in all. The children numbered their papers at the direction of the teacher, then the test began. "Cough," said the teacher. "I cough when I have a cold. Cough." That was word number one. She did the same thing with each word, walking up and down the rows, either because of nervousness or to make sure the kids didn't cheat.

Finally the test was over, and the kids exchanged papers and the teacher once more called out the words and spelled each one aloud. When that was over, and the papers handed back to their owners, the teacher asked, "How many got a hundred?" Several hands went up. "Those of you who got a hundred and know that you know how to spell all the words may come up to the desk and get your star to put on the chart." With much excitement, the "star" pupils accomplished this, with some counting the number of stars they had on the chart, etc. After quiet reigned again, the teacher pointed out to the rest of the class that they, too, could get stars if they would get hundreds.

I looked at the chart. It had many gold stars on it, but there were many blank spaces on it too. What about those kids who simply never could get all the words right? They never discovered gold. Neither did they learn to spell. Neither do millions of other children. Why not?

That is one of the questions of the century, but it needn't be. The answer seems obvious as heck to me: We don't teach spelling. We give kids lists of words and expect them to become excited about them and learn them. Whoever got excited about learning spelling? Excited about taking tests, yes, but not because they liked them. Excited either because they knew they'd get a hundred or because they knew they would fail and would have to write each word forty times each!

I can just hear the teachers saying, "He doesn't know what he's talking about. I might have a child write a word three or five times, but certainly never *forty* times." I'll admit that three or five times is not as idiotic as forty times, but I must ask teachers in general what has been accomplished by having a youngster write those misspelled words even three or five times? Have we developed a nation of better spellers? The evidence shows just the opposite.

There are scores and maybe hundreds of techniques used to teach kids to spell correctly, yet in spelling we are going *downward*. Evidently something must be wrong with the way we are teaching. Boy, I'll say there is! Go into nearly any classroom in the elementary school and you will find the kids *hating* spelling —most of the time. There are always a few cute little girls and a few smart boys who like it because they can do well in it, but even these say they sort of only endure it, because they already know how to spell all the words given for that week. Yet the teacher insists that they go through all the idiotic motions of learning how to spell them again.

Here's an example. A third-grade class had eleven spelling words given it as the week's work in spelling, just a mite over two words a day, on the average. I asked the teacher if she had any good spellers in the room, and she readily and happily told me yes, there were several, and proceeded to name them and point them out. You see, I was laying a trap for her. I then asked her if these kids (it was on a Monday) could get a hundred on a test today if she were to give it. "Oh, yes," she said brightly, "I'm sure they already know how to spell the words." Well, *damn* it! I didn't say that to her face you understand, but I should have, and would have, but my job, again, is not to tell the supervising teacher how to teach. But I jumped all over the student teacher later when I learned that she, after several weeks with the supervising teacher, was beginning to think just like that non-dynamo.

At the time that I was talking with the regular teacher, she told me more about what these children would be doing with the spelling words for that week. "Today," she continued, "they would be practicing alphabetizing the words. On Tuesday they would syllabicate the words and also put in accents. On Wednesday they would practice their dictionary skills, putting in the diacritical markings and also have that famous pretest. On Thursday they would write homonyms, synonyms, and antonyms. Then on Friday they would take the test and all would write the words in sentences as a part of the test. Oh, yes, those kids who got hundreds on Wednesday would not have to take the test on Friday."

Now, I submit to you, that there could hardly be found a more clever way of killing any desire to learn to spell than what this teacher was doing, but one of the damnable things about it is that she was doing exactly what the textbook ordered. And that particular book is a well-known and often-used book all over the country. Who, then, is making lousy poor spellers of our kids, I ask you?

The other night as my daughter was being shooed off to bed, she suddenly remembered that she had homework to do. "What is it?" we asked. "Spelling," she said. "What's the matter, don't you know how to spell?" I asked. "Yes, but I have to put the dumb words into syllables," she said. It turned out that she knew how to spell them all and had known how when the teacher wrote them on the board. (I think this partirular teacher wants to impress visitors in her room. She writes everything on the board.) Anyway, we decided that she should get up earlier in the morning and do them.

After the girl had gone upstairs, I suggested to my wife that we send a note to the teacher the next morning and tell her that inasmuch as our girl knew how to spell the words, that we had decided not to have her go through the syllabication process with each of the fifteen words. My wife, being more tender-hearted than I, and having more sense than I, said no. There was no point in antagonizing the teacher and making life hard on the child. I said, "What do you mean, making life hard on the child? She's getting to hate everything about school except recess and gym. She's bored to death!" My wife agreed with me in part about the girl being bored, but said that this was better than having the teacher down on her all the time and the other kids tormenting her about not having done her work. Naturally, I agreed with my wife.

There is another aspect of the teaching of spelling which makes me see red and makes me wonder about some of our moronic practices in this regard. Recently I was watching a second-grade spelling class in action studying their six words for the week. I could hardly contain myself. Here were these smart second-graders who could tell you all kinds of things that are happening on TV, who can pick up jingles with the greatest of ease, who can watch a movie on TV and play jacks, monopoly, etc., at the same time, and talk with each other and listen to their parents' conversation—do all these kinds of things, yet be given *six* spelling words to learn in five days. The idiocy of school people! Or those fifteen spelling words my daughter was given one week to study, when she already knew how to spell them. It makes me want to throw a rock at somebody. How did we ever get to be such idiots? In a little bit I'm going to tell you about some amazing and highly interesting things we are doing in spelling; then you will begin to understand why these traditional, tried, and untrue methods our kids are being subjected to throw me into such a tizzy.

But I must first talk a little bit about what we do to kids

in mathematics. It seem to me that we teach math, spelling, and reading in about the same idiotic way. It's always a one-number-plus-another-number kind of thing, or one-letter-plus-another-letter, and one-word-and-another-word affair in spelling, and reading. What if we had made our kids learn to talk in this manner? Where would we all be if this had been the kind of thing we all had encountered in the original learning-to-talk process? We probably would still be in the learning-to-talk process.

So what do we do in school? We give kids things that they already know how to do and expect them to be interested in school. Or we give them stuff that is over their heads, then bawl them out and/or flunk them for not doing the work. How many times have we all seen kids make careless mistakes in math, for example, because they hurry to get through the stuff they already know so they could get on to something which was interesting to them? A while back, my boy announced that he was going to get an F in math on his report card. "Why?" we asked. "Because I forgot to label my answers on the test." "Well, did you know how to do the problems?" we asked. "Oh sure, they're easy. Everybody knows how to do those." "Why didn't you label them?" we asked. "Because I was in a hurry to get out to recess," he said, "and forgot."

We talked with the teacher about the test, etc. Yes, he had given the boy an F on the test, but the report card grade would only be a D1. That means that the boy was working up to capacity but doing poor work. In reality, it meant that the boy was a poor labeler of math problems when he was in a hurry. The teacher admitted that the boy knew how to do the work, "But he will just have to learn to follow directions." Well, we want our boy to follow directions, and that is important in life, but we doubted, and still do, that at this particular time the lack of labeling was worthy of a D. The D1, you understand, meant that the boy was doing poor work, and that it was as much as he was capable of doing. Somebody or something was lying.

The other night a woman called me on the telephone to ask me what she should do about a situation. She said her son had never been too good a student and the teacher was trying to help the boy. I said that's good, but why call me? (I was polite about it, of course.) She said it was because math was the only thing he was good in, but now the teacher is making the boy hate that. "Why, what is he doing?" I asked. She told me.

"For homework that night the boy had been assigned fifty problems to do, and he hated it," she said. "I don't blame him a cockeyed bit," I said. "Tell him not to do all fifty of them. But does he know how to do them?" I asked. Sure, the boy knew how to do them: they were simple problems and none of them required any reading except of the numbers. (We know there are more than oodles of kids who can do math quite well if they don't have to read the problems.) "On second thought," I said, "tell him not to do any of them. Instead, you send a note back to the teacher tomorrow morning telling him your boy knows those problems, and to please give him something worthwhile to do." (You see, I can be awfully brave about telling other people what to do with their kids.)

The mother thought about this for a bit and we talked further. She decided to do as I had suggested, but of course, with a little more finesse. That was all right with me. I had just wanted to make it emphatic that she should do *something*. She did something. She went to see the teacher and he, in his most righteous tones (the mother told me later), said that every pupil in the class had been given that assignment, and that every pupil in the class was expected to complete it. Those who did not do it would simply be given more the next day, and more would be added each day until the work was done. "I don't play favorites," the teacher had said virtuously. "The assignment given to one child is given to all of the children."

And after all that lip service we give to individual differences! And after all those taxes we pay to get good teachers! It makes one want to rise up and give someone a mean look. Two, even.

So the mother went to see the principal. The teacher didn't like that; neither did the principal. He reminded the mother that her son Joe wasn't a good student and the teacher was merely trying to help the boy. This statement brought forth some choice remarks from Joe's mother about the school and its policies and especially its teachers. Whereupon the principal said that he would talk with the teacher and see what could be done. He did, but in the meantime, Joe's teacher made a few remarks of his own about parents who kept coming to the school and trying to run it. Joe was embarrassed in front of the whole class. That night he begged his mother not to do anything more about it. The mother did, however, but quietly. She talked with the principal again, and that time he spent fifteen minutes explaining to her that the teacher was attempting to get all of the students up to grade level, and that he was really concerned about Joe, and would do everything he (the teacher) could to help Joe attain and do grade level work.

The mother wanted to know how giving Joe fifty problems that he already knew how to do would help, especially when the whole darned class was getting exactly the same stuff. The principal said that the teacher "was following the outlined procedures which had been developed by a team of experts," and that if she would just be patient, she could rest assured that this would prove successful in Joe's case. Wow! Look, Look! See, See! See the Big Runaround!

The principal thought he clinched his point by reminding the mother that "after all, these books *are* written by people who have been working in mathematics for many years and have been writing books about it for a long time. They know their business."

What utter hogwash that is. I happen to know that many of the elementary textbooks, whether they be about math, reading, or basket weaving, are written by college professors teaching those subjects and who have not been in an elementary classroom since they graduated from grammar school. Furthermore, many of those guys (and gals) write because they are forced to or lose their jobs. "Publish or perish," you know. So instead of themselves perishing, they punish little kids by writing textbooks for them and putting in them everything they know. Well, that might be a *little* unfair to them.

But Joe's mother, feeling sorry for her son, ceased and desisted in her efforts to correct an outrageous practice, and Joe was not embarrassed very much more by the teacher. Better not to learn than to be embarrassed. Quoth the raven, "Evermore." Joe had learned one lesson, however. He quit complaining.

Now, I want you to know that I believe that the assigning of fifty or more math problems for one night's work is not too much, but even possibly far too little. Indeed, one of the *big* reasons our people over the centuries have *not* learned is because we have given too few or too little, not too much. But, we have developed the wrong principles of learning with what we have given. To repeat what I said before: "Where little is given, little is learned; where much is given, much more will be learned." But giving it in the traditional way, as for example the way we usually present math, spelling, reading, and foreign languages, is to deny the true principles of learning. Our out-of-school methods of learning often excel our in-school learning philosophy. Remember what that fellow on the National Council for the Disadvantaged said: "Teach your children all you can before they enter school, because once they start school, they begin to lose." Well, that's the way *I* said what he had hinted at. He actually said: "Every child who enters school becomes disadvantaged." What a ringing indictment against schools and organizations which purport to foster schooling! Verily, I believe it.

Verily, I know it, too! I know it because I have been able to put into action the principle of, "Where much is given, much more will be learned." I have come to believe, as have many others, that learning is a slow process because teaching is a slow process. Teaching is slow because we do not expect enough of our students in school. Traditional teaching methods have choked us; are still choking us as much today as they were fifty years ago. True learning techniques are smothered by them. Yet has there ever been a time in the history of mankind when there has been a more pressing need for greater learning at a faster rate? It is unthinkable that we should be forced to plod along through the learning process at the same rate at which our ancestors went. The horse-and-buggy days are still with us in the "schools of learning." In the learning skills such as reading, spelling and math in the elementary grades we move no faster than did those of fifty to a hundred years ago. Witness the six spelling words a week, the two pages of reading a day, the low math assignment per day, and even the teaching of a foreign language. (See the chapter devoted to the teaching of foreign languages.)

Chapter VI

New Brain Potential in Math and Spelling

The big problem with the special math teacher was herself—she could not keep those fifth-grade children supplied with enough math problems! She gave them five hundred problems a week and she felt that was all the time she could devote to selecting the problems and duplicating enough for all twenty-eight children in her class.

The special spelling teacher had a similar problem. She just could not, she said, give the second-, third-, and fourth-grade children with whom she was working more than six hundred spelling words a week! And the grading of them! Both the math and the spelling teachers wearied of the grading process until they had the pupils participate in this process.

Ah, you say, but the math book only calls for fifty to eighty problems per week. 'Tis so, and as a result, look where we are in math. The kids only do that many, or fewer, while the brain goes on to greater things.

"And look, you nut," you say to me, "the spelling book only calls for six to twenty-five words weekly." Yeah, that's right, but who ever decided that the human brain should be so limited in that manner? Surely the minds that can send rockets, voices, and pictures hundreds of thousands of miles into space can ferret out the intricacies of more than one to five spelling words a day!

A group of us decided that it could be done. We had already taught hundreds of children to read at very high speeds and some of them had achieved truly amazing speeds of reading with good comprehension. Indeed, they made national headlines with their high speeds in reading.

The successes which we achieved in this program tended to cause our imaginations to expand. We began to wonder about other subject areas. Could children be taught effectively in other areas of learning, using techniques similar to those used in teaching rapid reading? We reasoned thusly: Kids have been taught to spell in much the same way they were taught to read, i.e., one sound, or one letter, or one word, at a time. They were taught math similarly, i.e., one number plus another number equals another number, etc. As we watched both children and adults perform marvelously in reading, our belief was strengthened that the same newly discovered principles of teaching and learning could be applied to these other areas of learning as well.

I must digress for a moment at this point and remind us again that the principles and concepts which have been used over the centuries in the teaching of reading, mathematics, and spelling have not been highly successful. We have not produced a nation of *good* spellers, or *good* readers, or *good* mathematicians. Oh, we've gone to the moon and we've made great advances in the sciences in which mathematics plays a heavy part, but that's been done by a very small number of people. Most of us, by our own admission, are poor in math. Isn't that right, you parents who have trouble helping your own kids do their math assignments? The recent emphasis given to our school situation in this respect by the president of the United States and by the U.S. commissioner of education have underscored the regrettable conditions now existing.

In short, it seems logical to assume that the general and specific methods used in teaching the vital school subjects need to be strongly revised. A noted speaker recently told a group of teachers and parents that we do not read any faster or any better than did the educated classes of people of two hundred years ago.

This statement might be debatable, but the point he was making, and I thought it was a good one, was that our reading ability as a nation is very low and has not improved greatly over the years. Yet the material we have to read has increased a hundredfold at least in those years. Do we assign school pupils more math problems or more spelling words now than we did fifty or a hundred years ago? As I ponder this thought, I am struck again with the apparent stupidity of the idea that we expect today's fourth-grader to learn to spell only three to four words a day! Also, that we expect him to read no more than one or two reading textbooks in nine months' time. Think of it! It takes him from four and one-half months to nine months to read one textbook. The thought makes reason stare!

All right, so we became convinced that other subject areas could be taught in the same way we were teaching kids and adults to read rapidly and with good to excellent comprehension. We began experimenting, first with spelling then with mathematics. The kids *loved* these special periods when they could learn fast. They even volunteered to stay after school for *two hours* twice a week to help carry on this project. These were kids in the second through the sixth grades. Even now, as I write this, one of my teachers has a group of second-grade children meeting during the noon hour to study math and spelling in this manner. None of them has to attend. It is strictly voluntary yet she has a full class of them with more wanting to join. It's marvelous! In these classes the children beg the special teachers to stay longer and to start earlier.

As our efforts at teaching rapid math and rapid spelling progressed and met with success, our imaginations continued to grow. If the mind is capable of doing things like this, can it do more? In an organist, for example, uses both hands and both feet at the same time and is simultaneously reading at least two staffs of notes across the page at once, and is at the same time observing the musical signs along the way, and is also remembering the notes where the sharps and flats are to be played, *and* is watching the conductor or chorister, and perhaps himself singing—if the organist can do all of this, we said, can we learn in two academic areas such as math and spelling, at the same time?

We decided to combine "rapid math" and "rapid spelling." We counseled among ourselves in this way: The more we experience the more we learn. If a child experiences twenty spelling words a week, he will learn twenty or fewer. If he experiences six hundred a week, then will he not learn several hundred more than twenty? We thought the same about math problems. We decided to try. What was there to lose?

Essentially the same techniques which had produced highly skilled readers were used in teaching math and spelling. We prepared literally hundreds of very simple spelling words and math problems and placed them at odd angles on the pages. We had previously learned that children often prefer to look at words and numbers at angles different from the usual or "regular" way, and that often they can see better when their materials are turned in different directions from those generally taught and used. (See pages 81-82.)

In the beginning the math problems were presented with the answers already given. Later the answers were removed and the same and different problems presented. We discussed at length with the children the various ways of looking at the pages containing words and numbers. We explained to them that there are other ways of looking at pages than from left to right, just as we had done in teaching them to read rapidly. We told them that some of them could see an entire page clearly, while others could see only parts of pages at a glance. Still others could see best in the manner in which they had originally been taught. We proceeded to give the following instructions:

1. See the words (problems) in any way you wish: across the page, down, down and up, diagonally, zigzag, etc.
2. See as much of the page, or as many of the words (problems) as you can at one glance.
3. Do not (repeat), do *not* try to understand any of them. See them as *fast* as you can and as many of them as you can in *five* seconds. Do not try to spell the words or do the problems yet. We will do that later.

This process was followed for three to five periods with no attempt being made on the part of the teachers to have the children understand what they were seeing. Of course it was difficult for the children *not* to try to spell some of the words or do some of the problems, but seeing all of the "blocks of print" with *no comprehension* was stressed. We have to help get a person in the habit of seeing fast first, then move him into comprehension. We were also emphasizing the concept of seeing

hang boss bell dance glass fence

race cost

sell socks string

police loud hung electric receive

below

nothing pack kiss finger decide

fill camel

stocking arrow stack block

shell sung circus

slow strong till pound

tack rice neck evening

wail cloud brick

music tomorrow interesting tall

king luck since pocket mouth sting

cover mountain ill wing

cabin mouse hall bowl

cross thick during kick recess follow

swing

hanging south sound truck

proud stuck spill track

fire $\frac{8}{14}$ light game $\frac{8}{17}$ dark $\frac{8}{18}$ bark $\frac{8}{10}$ farm $\frac{8}{11}$

$\frac{8}{15}$ $\frac{8}{16}$ are $\frac{8}{14}$

snake $\frac{8}{13}$ car $\frac{8}{15}$ large grade $\frac{8}{16}$ bright barn $\frac{2}{8}$

$\frac{2}{12}$ $\frac{8}{17}$

$\frac{8}{4}$ $\frac{2}{7}$ night $\frac{8}{16}$ late $\frac{8}{5}$ $\frac{8}{12}$ written far fight $\frac{8}{9}$

$\frac{2}{4}$ $\frac{2}{4}$ $\frac{2}{4}$ rose $\frac{2}{6}$ wrote hard made $\frac{2}{11}$ might party $\frac{2}{12}$

$\frac{2}{5}$ yard $\frac{2}{5}$ $\frac{2}{3}$ se farm home high soon

$\frac{2}{8}$ now $\frac{2}{13}$ ground

star $\frac{2}{8}$ catch $\frac{2}{7}$ found $\frac{6}{10}$ three $\frac{2}{15}$ store $\frac{2}{17}$

$\frac{2}{9}$ while $\frac{2}{6}$ like each part child who know

watch $\frac{2}{9}$ talk $\frac{2}{14}$ wait $\frac{2}{12}$ thank $\frac{2}{13}$ more math

start sang spring $\frac{2}{6}$ $\frac{2}{7}$ kitten $\frac{2}{10}$ these walk smoke

bring $\frac{2}{13}$ those owl round

shoe kept dish milk bite loud

what chicken children

which shoot please week cook chair

dear poor seed street goes town

sheep food flower nice

cake clothes zoo clock race dance

corn card color place would

face ice 100%

in "wholes" rather than in "pieces."

Had we not previously been amazed at what children had accomplished in rapid reading we would certainly have been amazed now. Many of the youngsters found they could see an entire page at a time; others could see in odd directions, while still others could see no more than they had been taught to see in their regular classes in spelling and math. How often, for example, does a teacher say to a pupil, "Look at the problem as a whole instead of the individual numbers?" Or how often does the teacher ask the children to see the spelling words in their entirety? Never! Invariably, the word is broken down into its individual parts, especially if there has been training in syllabication. But we only have to tell children they can do certain things, and allow them to do them, and they astound us with their accomplishments. But we have to believe in them enough to allow them to try.

After a few days of just "seeing" the words and pushing for faster speeds, we began working on understanding:

4. Now, without slowing down, try to understand some of what you are seeing. Remember, do not slow down, but try to understand (spell or do) just one or two words (problems). Can you see the page(s) as many times in three seconds now and understand one or two things, as you did before when you were understanding nothing? "Ready, go!"

(Some of the children had found it seemingly impossible *not* to understand some of the words or problems and had already been doing so before they had been instructed to do it. This did not disturb us unless they were going very slowly. One of the purposes in having them "see fast" was to try to get them out of the habit of vocalizing or "sub"-vocalizing each letter or word or number. Persons who have to "hear" or "see" the words or numbers in their minds go almost as slowly as they would if they were saying them aloud. This is true in reading, spelling, or "arithmetic-ing.")

5. Go over the same page(s) again and this time, without slowing down, try to understand (spell the words or do

the problems) one or two more than you did before. Remember, you are to understand only a few now. Remember, also, that you are to look at them in any way you can see them best, i.e., from left to right or right to left, straight down, zigzag, etc. For 15 seconds, ready, Go! (The time varied, depending on what the teacher felt would be most advantageous for the class at a given time. However, in these early stages no more than 20 to 30 seconds were allowed.)

6. (Fourth or fifth day) We began, as we do each period, with warmup exercises, practicing for speed and breadth of vision only and with no effort at comprehending. After two or three 10-to-20-second "warmups" we again called for "just a little comprehension or understanding," going over the same material several times. With each additional time we asked for additional understanding. For example, we asked the youngsters to observe more word forms, or more number combinations each time without losing what they had already gained. As we progressed, or rather as the kids progressed, we had to cut down the number of seconds allowed to look over the material, and to begin supplying more and more problems and words. They were beginning to recognize wholes in words and in numbers.

This process continued from day to day, with each period beginning with the "warmups," then moving into more and better understanding. We were trying to help them develop habits of seeing and comprehending more at a time. We believed that these habits would carry over into other activities. (I will comment further on this aspect of the program a little later.) In the meantime, what fun we were having! And the kids were, too.

Because of the variations in scheduling in the different schools where our teachers were working with the children, some of the classes were held twice a week for six weeks; some three times a week for six weeks, and one was conducted only once a week for sixteen weeks. If any differences could be noticed in the results, those classes which met three times a week would have a slight edge. We could not help but wish that the classes had been held more often and for a longer period of time. One of the school principals, commenting before a P.T.A. group on the progress which had been made in her school, said, "These children have been in these programs for only six weeks. Just think of what they might accomplish had they nine months of this kind of training. We are looking forward now to next September so we can start at the beginning and really have an exciting time."

And truly, truly, the results we obtained were interesting and exciting:

1. Above all, the kids were enthusiastic about this "new kind" of math and spelling. They awaited eagerly the arrival of the special teachers, and bemoaned their leaving at the end of the period. One of the teachers, whom I have mentioned before, had to meet with her group of second-, third-, and fourth-graders after school because of scheduling difficulties. They met for two hours *after* school. Imagine! Children voluntarily remaining for two hours *after* school to study *spelling!* Ridiculous; but they did. The teacher said again and again that one of her problems was getting the children to go home so she could leave at five o'clock to fix her husband's dinner. They loved what they were doing because they were experiencing a kind of success not experienced before by any of them: They were learning hundreds and thousands of words.

2. What did they learn? To *like* learning. Thousands of math problems a month and thousands of words. Many of the children were able to do three or four math problems at one time, and to spell more than one word at a time. That is, while writing one word they could spell another and still another orally. It was a fascinating thing. And they only needed a few seconds in which to look over a whole page, then wanted to be tested on the material thereon. And that material, remember, contained scores and hundreds of spelling words and math problems.

We should not be too surprised, however. Consider what the organist does in his regular playing of the organ. He must perform about fifteen or sixteen or more activities at the same time, and we think nothing of him doing it. He's supposed to do that, we say. He is trained to do it. Then why don't we train ourselves to do a lot of other things which will bring about greater learning and greater pleasure? Like learning math in a fun way and spelling too? We *are* kind of dumb, aren't we, when we stop to think about it.

3. Of interest to us was the fact that a total of seven children in two fifth- and sixth-grade classes had previously been given several weeks of instruction in rapid reading before the spelling and math programs were begun. These seven youngsters, without exception, progressed faster in the beginning than did the others, and four of the seven were among the top ten in both the spelling and the math programs when these classes came to a close.

4. Another point of interest and one, I feel, of real significance, was the experience of the spelling class that met after school for two hours twice a week. In the next to the last class meeting of the group the teacher brought a stack of storybooks and passed them among the children, making no comment over them, and one of the children suggested that "we read these like we did our spelling—fast." The teacher agreed (that's what she had in mind in bringing the books) and administered several "tests" or timings from these books. The teacher had chosen the books carefully with an eye to grade level and had passed them out to the children accordingly. This interesting fact appeared: These children, with no instruction having been given them in rapid reading, read from three hundred to four thousand words a minute with good to excellent comprehension. The lowest score was made by a second-grader who was a little below average in I.Q., and the highest score was made by a fourth-grader. The norm in reading rates for second-graders is about eighty words a minute, while for fourth-graders the norm is about one hundred and thirty-five words per minute.

The teacher and the kids could hardly wait to tell of their experiences. This was real learning! And when others found they could do both math and spelling at the same time, and do literally gobs of math problems in a matter of minutes, they went crazy. They asked for more! They weren't satisfied. What else could they do? A group of second-graders meeting during the noon hour, found that five hundred math problems and spelling words a week were not enough for them, apparently. They asked their teacher for more and she said "No! I can't give you any more." "Then what are we going to do?" asked the kids. The teacher asked them if they would like to try including reading along with the math and the spelling. "Yea, yea," they shouted.

So now that crazy teacher is combining all three of the subjects. How it all will turn out we don't know yet, but I'm betting on the kids. Want to put up some money?

We became excited with these new possibilities. Our curiosity was aroused to a high pitch as we wondered how far this concept of learning could take us. Previously I had seen children and adults achieve extremely high rates on reading, with total recall. I had marveled again and again at the possibilities of human potential exhibited by these people, especially the younger ones. Now this, in math and spelling, and now maybe math, spelling, and reading combined. It seems that all we have to do is to tell our students they can do something like this and allow them to do it, then step aside so we don't stand in the way of their learning.

It gives one almost an awesome feeling as he observes phenomena such as those described above. Tremendous gifts are in store for us. We have but to reach out for them.

But how many of our so-called teachers are going to reach out for them? That teacher who gives her second-graders six words a week? That teacher who is told by her principal to follow her Guidebook and not deviate from it? That teacher who insists that every child be given the same assignment as all the others? Believe me, this kind of teaching is going on in the majority of our classrooms even as I write this.

And we are going to let it continue if we continue passive and allow the textbook companies to tell our teachers what, when, how, and why to teach. It will continue to happen as long as our school administrators have no better sense than to insist that the teachers use the textbook as the basis and

Bible for their teaching. There is nothing wrong with the Bible, but *it* is the Bible. The textbook is just another book and should be treated as such. That young lady who is attempting to teach three subjects at once has already tossed aside the textbooks as such. Oh, she uses them, but only to get materials to use because it's easier than making up all of those words and problems from out of her own head. That second-grade teacher who let her kids finish all of their books by Thanksgiving didn't think of the textbooks as "hallowed." They were just books to be used as rapidly as possible, then cast aside for more learning materials. And so on and so forth.

Someone is going to ask: "Well, just how were the kids given these math problems and spelling words in such great numbers?" Simple. They were given math problems with two and three digits down, and the same number of digits across to begin with. They were told, "Remember, try to see all of the numbers at once, or as many as possible at one time and not be concerned about the answers at first." In the beginning the answers were given with the problems. Later the answers were taken away, and still later the problems were enlarged and made more complicated. As the more complicated problems were introduced, answers were again provided, then later removed. Still later, new problems of the more complicated kind were added.

The kids loved the challenge. One of the things we had to be careful about, believe it or not, was not to give them too much time in which to do the problems and the spelling words. One teacher, who was new to the program, said to one group of students, "Now, I know that there are lots of problems and words here, and it will be too hard for you. I'm going to give you ten minutes in which to do these two pages, and you do as many as you can. Don't feel bad if you don't get them all finished." Bah! By the time the ten minutes were up the kids were using their papers for airplanes and whatnot. They were finished and tired of waiting for the ten minutes to expire. The teacher had certainly learned her lesson. The kids had learned how to learn.

We have done a mighty poor job of deciding what the

human mind is capable of doing. We have done an even worse job of analyzing the workings of the mind of the individual as such. But we have done a darned good job of selling to others our thoughts concerning our weaknesses and shortcomings. We have done such a good job of this that it is reflected directly in the guidebooks and instructions given the teachers. This is especially true with the so-called New Math. It has become a sort of sacred cow. It is supposed to show kids the *how* and the *why* of mathematics. Just how well it's doing this is still too early to tell. Many of the teachers swear by it; many of the parents swear *at* it.

It might or might not be working, but thus far there has been no real report that it has brought into existence more mathematicians. Nor has it caused more kids to like math. And if they don't like it, they don't do well in it. The New Math is a slow, tedious process for many youngsters *and* their parents. It is well known for its logical step-by-step process. When finished with a problem, a youngster is supposed to understand just *why* two times two is five, or four, or whatever it is he is supposed to know *why* about.

But the whole darned process is too slow. In this step-by-step procedure, *whose* step are we supposed to follow? And how big should the step be? And in which direction? Should it be a giant step or a dwarf step? What about the boy or girl who can see through the intricacies of the whole problem at once, but has to slow down for all the curves? Well, he just slows down and does what all the other kids are doing. The same number of problems, the same amount of time in which to do them, and the same kinds of work. Don't think I'm guessing or just shooting in the dark. I've seen it happen, I'll bet, at least umpteen hundred times. What does it do to the kids? Most of them still hate math just like their parents did before them, and the majority are reacting to it just like their parents and grandparents did—negatively.

And why not? For years we've been at the job of slowing down the minds of our kids. The human being is a fast thinker. Put him in an emergency situation and his reactions are pure speed. Put him in a math class and you make a dumbbell out of him. It's not because he can't think straight and fast and logically that we decide he's a dummy in math: It's because we try to make him think in someone else's programmed manner of thinking. If he does not react exactly like the book and/or how the teacher has indicated, we down him mentally. In other words, if we can't program him in the way we want, he's "just no good" in math.

How many millions of parents have told their kids that they (the parents) were not any good at math, and that's why the kids are not? Well, right away the kids decide that that's the way it is or it will be with them. And they don't learn. They don't have to; it's already been decided for them. In nearly every class I visit I am told by the teacher either that she has "the low group," or that there are "many who should not be in this class" because they are just slow learners in math. Who can blame the kids? They are told to go slowly, be correct in their thinking and figuring, and if they make a mistake they are graded down in their work. It's a sure-fire way to get them to dislike math and do poorly in it.

And you know what? We've been doing it for a thousand years or so and are still doing it! How much longer (another millennium?) will we go on being such dunderheads? There is a great deal being said nowadays about a thing called the "flow chart." It's a new gimmick, relatively speaking, for getting people to think in a straight line, i.e., from one point to another, to the next, etc. It's supposed to help us to think logically, from step to step. Again, whose step? Giant or dwarf? Well, I can tell you. It's in the step of the person who devised it, or the teacher who is using it. We will wind up just as we have over the centuries—robots in math. The robots get the A's and we others get the F's. "We others" come to hate math and continue to be glad when the math class is over.

Not so those kids in those special math-spelling classes! They take all they can get and ask for more. They run the teachers ragged preparing more and newer materials. "But" you say "what's going to happen to those kids when they get into a class where the teacher is of a different opinion and follows the rules of the book?" Oh I've been asked this question a few hundred times by college students who are preparing to teach, and by parents whose kids are having such fun in these special classes. I tell them, "At least the kids are having *one* year of fun. Let the next year's teacher worry about what the kids are going to be doing then. Maybe they'll push some fool teacher into giving them something they can really use." Just think how much fun they'll have punishing that teacher! She will have to really dig to keep up with them. Remember, those kids can do several problems at once, can see through to the logical conclusion without having to follow the step-procedure so dearly loved by many. Won't they get a kick out of frustrating that teacher who wants things "done in an orderly way?" What a time they'll have!

And spelling? That's a laugh. Listen, there are those second-graders and third-graders right now who are getting more than five hundred spelling words a week. Do you know how many that is in one school year? Well, do some multiplying, and see if you don't get about ninety thousand! Where, now, are those "three thousand spelling demons" we hear about and see in the spelling textbooks, and in the textbooks used by college professors of education? Think of it. Twenty thousand words a year in spelling that these kids are getting and loving.

Now think of the textbook teacher and the second-grade kids who are "learning" six words a week. In a school year's time they will have studied 216 words. And who will have learned them? Well, some of the pupils, most of whom already knew how to spell them anyway. What a dreary prospect! But, blast it, that's the way it is in most of our schools. Who's going to change it? Not the teachers. They're afraid of losing their jobs. And they would. Not the school administrators nor the boards of education; it would cost too much money to change. Their main concern is to keep down expenses. And certainly not the publishers; they're making too much money publishing tripe and folderol. Not the parents; they're told not to meddle, but to let the running of the schools stay with those who have been trained to run them. So there it stands.

Chapter VII

The Fabulous Foreign Language Freak-Out

"Fantastic! Utterly fantastic!" So exclaimed a Spanish teacher who had just retired from teaching. Then she added: "What in the world have I been doing for the past twenty-five years?"

She had just watched a group of young people, mostly of elementary school age, read rapidly in Spanish and English. They were reading several thousand words a minute in both languages after only weeks of instruction.

Another Spanish teacher of six years experience asked herself out loud: "Have my six years of teaching been wasted?" These kids had done something that was heretofore thought impossible. They had learned to read a foreign language, and to read it rapidly, in a very short period of time. It was indeed remarkable when compared with the tired and shoddy way in which foreign languages are usually taught in this country.

Truly, we have faked the teaching of foreign languages in our high schools. What a mess! And the piddling inane fooling around with them that we have done in the elementary schools is a shame and a disgrace and would be better forgotten about. But burying our heads in the sand about this would not help the situation. After October of 1957 we all made a mad dash to get on the bandwagon and start teaching foreign languages, math, physics, chemistry, etc., in our schools with a fervor heretofore unknown. We were going to try to catch up with the Russians in whatever they were doing better than we. Maybe we succeeded in some things; maybe not in others.

Certain it is that we made utter fools of ourselves. We spent great gobs of money on fancy equipment that was supposed to help speed up the teaching and learning of foreign languages.

It didn't. Most high school students who study a language wind up speaking or reading a few simple sentences in it, and that's all. Recently I visited in a large high school which prides itself on being one of the best in that state. There was a "language laboratory" in the school, with all kinds of tapes, recorders, earphones, private booths—one for each student—the whole works. The head of the language department showed me around through the rooms with evident pride. Then I asked that disturbing question which I had asked before in other schools, "Do you find that this really does help the students learn the languages better than what you were doing before?"

The teacher glanced over his shoulder as though he thought the principal were listening at the keyhole, then said, "Hell no. This is a lot of bunk. When we first got this stuff the kids were wild about it. Now that it's old and the novelty has worn off, they could care less about it. I feel the same way about it."

Thousands of dollars had been spent on this "stuff." It was of little value to the students when it was purchased, and even less now.

So a lot of dollars were wasted there, and several million all over the country. But even before it was wasted, what was being produced in foreign language classes in high school? Not much, I'll tell you. I have studied foreign languages myself. I have had four children of my own go through them, and I have visited many such classes over the years. Most of them are fakes and we really ought to label them as such. They needn't be, but that's what they are, except for the occasional student who is really interested in pursuing the language as a special interest. And the reason they are a fake is the way we go about teaching them. It is a slow, tedious, torturous procedure, and most of the kids don't learn enough to make it worthwhile. By that I mean the students can't put it to use except to try to impress their classmates with a smattering of simple, often mispronounced words.

The situation is much the same, and sometimes worse, on the college level. Most college students shy away from foreign languages as if they were the plague. The languages, I mean. And they almost are, for those students who are not planning to major in that field. Again, why not? The way the languages are taught is a crime and enough to make anyone duck when he sees them coming at him; so most students, who can, do duck them. But many colleges require at least two years of a foreign language for graduation. Many colleges also require two years of a language in high school for college entrance. So— one way or another, we catch the students in a net of poorly taught foreign languages, and when they finish their two years in these courses, then what? Do they know how to speak them? No. Do they know how to read them? No. What *do* they know about them? Nothing much. They didn't want to take them in the first place, and after two years of learning little or nothing that would help them, they are glad to forget what little they did learn. Big fake, again.

But wait, there is still more to the story. There is the college which says to the student that if he wishes to graduate from that institution with a B.A. degree, he must take at least two years of a foreign language, and pass them, of course. Or if he wishes, he may elect to work toward a B.S. degree, in which case he need not take any foreign languages, but take some additional courses in an area of his or the college's choosing. So what do you think happens? That's right; when given the choice, most students get a B.S. degree. And where does that leave the foreign language department of the college? Fighting for students so that it may justify its existence.

Big fake, again.

Then comes the day when the college decides that it can no longer justify the difference it has maintained exists between the B.A. degree and the B.S. degree. Why should the foreign language requirement make the difference in the kind of degree a person gets? Since it can't really justify the difference, the college votes out the foreign language requirement entirely, much to the delight of the students, and much to the consternation of the foreign language faculty. That department begins to fade out. Only majors in the languages now take the courses. In the numerous small colleges this means that perhaps there will be no more than one or two students a year, and maybe not that many. Then watch out!

These few majors in due time are sent out to teach, first in student teaching, then into regular jobs. The un-fun is repeated. The high school students become the victims of these almost-stragglers. They may or may not know a great deal about the language they are trying to teach. You see, whether they come from a small or a large institution, if they have managed to squeak by with a C average, they graduate and go into the high schools to teach. I know of some right now who are there blithely showing off their ignorance to their students.

And now we're coming down to the ridiculous nub of the situation. The teachers teach the way *they* were taught in high school, not the way they were *taught* to teach while they were in college. No, not that. They teach the way they were taught while they were in *high school,* and in *grade school.* Then when they do their student teaching, this is emphasized again and again, so that when they begin their regular teaching, they teach just as they were shown how to teach. It's a terrible thing to do to them, and an even worse thing to do to the kids who are being taught in high school. They're the victims, and in time they victimize others when they begin their teaching.

Now wait a minute! I'm not kidding, nor am I exaggerating. It actually happens that way and as a result, we have the foreign language fake being repeated every year in thousands of classrooms. The teachers get paid for trying to teach the student something which is not learned. The school continues to spend money for a bunch of expensive equipment that is not used, and when it is used, it produces nothing more than what was produced before Sputnik. The kids don't learn the languages, the college perpetuates the farce, and the vicious circle continues forever and anon. We've got to stop it, and we can just by using some common sense. I'll tell you how in a little bit. (You see, I have an answer for everything!) But right now, I must direct your attention back to the sad and farcical attempts to teach foreign languages in the elementary schools.

We really must have been more than stupid to let somebody lure us into attempting to teach foreign languages to little kids. Oh, wait a minute! I'm not saying it can't be done or shouldn't be done. On the contrary; it *should* be done but the deplorable methods coming from the asinine philosophy behind them, are enough to make me cry. There was that *thing* called FLES (Foreign Languages in the Elementary School) that nearly wrecked us. We went all out for it in our determination to expose early our little children to a foreign language, thinking that if we did we would be making it a lot easier for them later on to really study the languages, and also give them a real desire to learn one or more. "After all," we said, "isn't that what they do in Europe, and don't the kids grow up knowing how to speak several languages?"

Right! That's absolutely correct. They do grow up knowing how to speak several languages. But . . . they study those languages every day for several years in a highly systematic way, and very diligently. They do not go about it in the piddling manner of many of our teachers in this country. Indeed, often the teachers themselves have only had a course or two in the language they play at teaching. Often the instruction they give lasts for ten to twenty minutes, with the children parroting back the words the teacher speaks. The periods of instruction are short and often sporadic, being slipped in between regularly scheduled subjects. It's plumb dumb of us to even think of comparing our sorry "program" of foreign languages for children with the more determined one developed by the European countries.

Furthermore, when the kids in Germany, for example, are taught English they have occasion to use it more or less daily, both in and out of the classroom. Not so when our American kids are barely exposed to a foreign language, such as German. Where can they use the few words they learn, and how can they use them anyway? In the processes used to teach the language the kids encounter so few that they learn too little to put them to adequate use, even if they had an outlet for them. Instead, when one consideres the silly approach to the teaching of the languages, it is little wonder that someone has not already blasted such teaching out of the schools long ago.

Here is an example of what I mean. Read it and be amazed and disgusted with our simplemindedness in this matter of our teaching foreign languages.

In a large "modern" high school, four sections of first-year Spanish were being taught. The teachers had gotten together and decided that they would "move along together" through the book. That is, they would all be teaching the same lesson the same day, etc. This they proceeded to do and by the end of the school year the four sections had covered ninety pages in the books. They had stayed together, which apparently was the major goal of the teachers. The students didn't mind, I suppose, since some of them didn't have to exert themselves a great deal, and others didn't have to exercise their minds but rarely and still received high grades in the course.

Now there are usually about 180 school days in a school year. *These students read, on the average, one half page a day during the school year!* How much Spanish do you suppose they learned in nine months' time? How could they *possibly* have learned much when they only encountered little? And in checking in two other high schools, one public and one private, I found that much the same kind of thing was expected of the students. Again, let me point out that where little is given, little will be learned; whereas, where much is given, much more will be learned. By the way, we were able to test several of these students for speed in words per minute as they read silently in Spanish. The average rate of seven of them was forty-five words per minute, which is about par for first-graders reading in English! Comprehension for these seven was poor in general, but we were not able to obtain exact comprehension scores on them.

As I think on this situation I develop a purple passion about our asininity regarding the teaching of foreign languages. It appears as though we surely have had a stupor of thought in this matter of teaching them. I cringe at the thought of the millions of hours we have wasted in what we have stupidly called teaching the languages.

Let me go back now to the two Spanish teachers who had just witnessed something really rare occuring in this area. They had seen a group of youngsters read in Spanish and English at high rates of speed after only six weeks of instruction and practice. But why shouldn't they have been able to do these things? Unlike the Spanish classes mentioned above who read one-half page a day, these pupils were reading scores and hundreds of pages daily. They were encountering not just a few dozen words a day, but rather thousands and thousands of words a day. They *had* to learn Spanish. It's just like the baby born in Spain. He hears thousands of words a day, so he learns to speak Spanish from scratch. It's a most natural thing, and we have not yet really learned our lesson well from it.

But we're making some progress, and exciting progress it is, too! That was the first group of youngsters, as far as we know, who had ever tried such a thing. They learned to read rapidly in English and they learned to read Spanish, and to read it rapidly. They had not had any previous instruction in the language.

Then we began to expand our horizons. Many of us have come to believe that the mind of man is capable of doing things far beyond and far greater than what we have allowed it to do. Learning to read a foreign language rapidly and one's native language rapidly at the same time seems impossible, but consider again the person who uses both hands and feet at the same time as he plays the organ. He is also reading at least two staffs of notes across the page at once, observing the musical signs along the way, remembering the notes where the sharps or flats are to be played, watching the conductor or chorister, and perhaps himself singing—all of these activities almost simultaneously. Why should we consider it impossible, then, to read silently in two languages rapidly, or work two or more math problems at the same time, or to spell two or more words at the same time? (Oh, I know that we only *write* one word at a time, or one number, but we can *learn* more than one at a time.)

To what extent can the brain be made to function in the field of foreign languages? Still feeling furious, concerned and frustrated about the way the languages are usually taught in school, I was able to interest some of my braver prospective teachers in some additional projects in this subject matter area. If we can teach kids to read rapidly in *one* foreign language and in their own language at the same time, can we teach people to read in two languages with which they are unfamiliar, and to read them rapidly? After many discussions about possibilities, methods, materials, etc., we tried. We chose 110 junior high, senior high, and college students for the experiment, and assigned two young teachers to each class. This was a nine-week program, with the classes meeting twice a week for about one hour each time. The methods we used were the same, in general, which we had used in teaching all of the other classes where we were trying to speed up the learning process. The materials, however, were arranged differently this time. We had learned from past experience with the Spanish and English experiment that when a person can see the translation immediately before him that he can "catch on" much more quickly to what is being said. We had also noted this kind of thing in connection with our work in rapid mathematics. That is, when the answers to the problems are already given, in the beginning, there was much more encouragement on the part of the pupil, and much faster learning.

We decided to do the same thing with the languages. This time we were teaching Spanish, English, and French. Using a story written originally in English, and having had our translators put it in Spanish and French, we placed the lines of the story in the following manner, taking some liberties with the structure or tense occasionally:

Un día ocurrie algo muy extraño   (Spanish)
Then one day something very strange
Puis, un jeur quelque chose très étrange   (French)

y muy graciose. Usted sabe que   (Spanish)
and funny happened. You know that
et amusante est arrivée. Vous savez qu'un   (French)

una ballena puede hacer una cosa que   (Spanish)
a whale can do one thing that
baleine peut faire une chose que   (French)

la mayoría de les peces y otres animales   (Spanish)
most of the fishes and other sea
la plupart des poissons et les autres   (French)

We gave the materials to the students enrolled in the program and told them to see the words in the story as rapidly as possible without attempting to understand anything, not even the English part. We also gave them some instructions concerning the way we see words, and that each person sees and responds differently. We told them they could look at the words in whatever manner they wished, or in whatever direction they wished. We gave them some possibilities of seeing, and how other people look at words, but that they were to use their own best way or ways in doing this. But in all of this, they were to go fast and without understanding.

After several periods of this kind of practice, we then began working toward comprehension, but only gradually, little by little. The response was extremely rewarding. Some of the students had already had some experience with one of the foreign languages and some had had no experience with either of them. After a while it seemed to make very little difference whether or not a person had already been somewhat familiar with the languages. Astounding progress was made, and in a matter of weeks some of the students could read rapidly in all three languages. I mean that they could read thousands of words a minute with good understanding. Why not? They were encountering thousands of words a day.

The materials we had given them to start with were of simple elementary grade level. Later we gave them some additional materials of a more difficult type, and encouraged them to start reading in their regular textbooks the way we were teaching them in the special classes. The students enjoyed this type of reading probably because they were making much faster progress than in their regular classes. Some did better in French than they did in Spanish, and with some it was the other way around. But they progressed beyond, and some far beyond, what we had anticipated.

The highest scores were made by the high school students, probably because they put in more actual time in practice. Of great interest to me and to several other people, was the fact that the slowest reader of them all was the one Spanish teacher who had enrolled in the course. She admitted that she had not practiced as much as she should have, but she, and we, felt that it was also because she was just too steeped in the way she had been teaching and the way she had been taught Spanish, and the way she had been taught to teach it. She read only about seven hundred words a minute in Spanish, and did very poorly in French. Others in her class read many times faster than did she, and with better understanding.

As I look again at the scores of these students in their reading, I grind my teeth down even further in anger and frustration at the damnable philosophy which prevails in most of our schools concerning the teaching, and the requirements, of foreign languages. In a matter of weeks we had students reading dozens of books in these languages. Yet what does the average high school do? Have the kids read 90 pages in 180 days! Think what *we* could have done in 180 days!

Well, you say, if you're so good, and what you did with the students was so great, why don't the high schools adopt these methods? The same reason the world has not adopted our form of democracy. It takes time to change people's habits of thinking and training. This Spanish teacher who took the course, for example, is not now teaching the way we did in those special classes. She's afraid of it. Do you suppose for one minute she wants her students to read better in Spanish than she does? Who's the teacher around here, anyway? And besides, she's not sure she can teach that way, but she is very secure in her old way. So that's that.

In the program I've been talking about, we did little or nothing about teaching the students to speak the languages. We knew we could teach the oral part very quickly after a person developed a large reading vocabulary. He is already familiar with the words, and by having him follow along on a tape, reading orally that which he has been reading silently, the words fell into place for him. The same type of materials are used for carrying on a conversation. When I think of the expanded comprehension, both silent and spoken, of this kind of teaching, the usual tripe which is taught pales into the twilight in its effectiveness.

A question now arises: Having shown that we can learn two foreign languages simultaneously, and read rapidly in three languages at once, should we stop there? Did we accidentally hit upon the maximum number of foreign languages with which this is possible, or is it perhaps possible to study more than two languages using this method? Just how far can we go, and how ridiculous can we get, in this teaching-learning process? Personally, I suggest that we push to the outer limits, if there are any. And I doubt seriously that there are. Unless we place some out there deliberately, as we have done in many cases in teaching, we cannot be stopped. Being stopped means being damned, and I don't want to be damned, even if I propose doing that to others who get in my way.

Dr. Herman Otto, writing in the *Saturday Review* for December 20, 1969, quoted a Russian writer, Ivan Yefremov, who had written that the brain of the human holds tremendous potential far beyond what we have yet experienced. Dr. Otto, in the article entitled "New Light on the Human Potential," quoted Dr. Yefremov as follows:

> The latest findings in anthropology, psychology, logic, and physiology show that the potential of the human mind is very great indeed. As soon as modern science gave us some understanding of the structure and work of the human brain, we were struck with its enormous reserve capacity. Man, under average conditions of work and life, uses only a small part of his thinking equipment. . . . If we were able to force our brain to work at only half its capacity, we could, without any difficulty whatever, learn forty languages, memorize the large Soviet Encyclopedia from cover to cover, and complete the required courses of dozens of colleges.

In further commenting on the above statement, Dr. Otto said: "The statement is hardly an exaggeration. It is the generally theoretical view of man's mental potentialities." Dr. Otto, incidentally, is the chairman of the National Center for the Exploration of Human Potential, in La Jolla, California. He "speaks as one having authority." He also hints strongly that what we teachers have done to little children is abominable in the learning process. We have held them back; we have cut back their creativity; we have convinced them that they cannot perform well in anything except play, and that their productivity can amount to nothing.

Did you note Dr. Yefremov's statement concerning the use of the brain as it relates to foreign languages? He said that with even half a brain we could easily learn forty languages if we wanted to. (Yeah, I know he didn't say *half* a brain, but could it mean the same thing if we were really using it?)

But what do we do? Take two years to piddle around with a foreign language and have nothing to show for it. That's one of the reasons I'm writing this book. I want to draw attention to the malicious malingering that is going on in the schools, and to suggest some changes. Modification Behavior, one might call it. That's a term making the rounds in education today. It means changing the way we act. That's a darned good idea. Let's change the way we act and do something sensible.

Or, as one fellow said, "Let's do *something,* even if it's wrong."

Chapter VIII

The Godless Classroom and The PTA

or Maybe We Should Celebrate Water-puppy Day

Listen, I don't mean that the PTA *took* God out of the classroom: Two or three people managed to legislate Him out. The PTA just *let* Him out, it being the milquetoast organization that it is. That organization does nothing except what the principal is willing to let it do. If the principal doesn't want God in the classroom, neither does the PTA, so there! Now, the PTA will campaign for anything from a constitutional convention (Is that the business of the PTA?) to fewer flies in the classroom, and if you don't respond favorably you'll be labeled unpatriotic. My wife was—labeled, I mean.

But religion and God it lets alone. During the hassle which resulted in the Supreme Court outlawing prayer and Bible reading in the school, do you know what *my* PTA was doing? It was waging a door-to-door campaign to raise money for a new water fountain in the school . . . a cold-water fountain, that is. When some of us suggested that the school board was supposed to purchase the fountain out of our tax money, we were asked if we didn't think children had a right to drink cool water just as much as anyone else.

Well, I certainly have no objections to anyone, not even children, drinking cold water. My mother-in-law drinks it all the time. But it did seem as though we might have devoted our energies toward bigger projects. I was even bold enough to venture the thought that God and moral and spiritual values should take priority over water fountains. The withering looks of the ladies put me in my place in no time at all. They were afraid to discuss religion. They told me so.

So God left the classroom. But we got a water fountain.

It's an odd thing about this nonsense of religion in the classroom. *Whose* no-religion, I wonder. A kindergarten teacher told me not long ago that she could not teach her children any kind of song dealing with religion except Negro spirituals. This order, she said, came from the superintendent himself. "What about Christmas songs?" I asked. "We can sing about Santa Claus, toys, the snow on the housetops, and Christmas goodies, but not about Bethlehem," she replied. There were tears in her eyes as she said it, but she went on to tell me that she does sneak in a silent prayer before lunch. Bless her heart. I admire her. I hope, though, that the principal doesn't find out she's doing that. He will have to stop her. After all, he will only be doing what he's told. He is not supposed to think for himself in matters of this kind. Neither is a puppet.

I am sure there must have been many local PTA groups that fought to keep God and prayer in the classroom. I don't know of any personally. I sincerely hope there were some, though. In the many local groups which I knew about there was nothing done. But they were active, I'll tell you. Yes, indeed! They were busy putting on suppers to raise money to cover the budgets the executive committees had decided upon. This was stern business. And what was this money to be used for? Well, let's see. Was it to be used to study the curriculum of the school? No, the curriculum was good enough as it was. We'd had it for several years and it was working fine. Was it to arrange for study groups to see how other school districts operate their schools? No, for again, didn't we already have a good principal and a good school? Was it to be used to hold classes in child development for the parents? No, of course not. All parents know how to rear children, and those who really need the classes would not come anyway. Was it to be used to pay the telephone expenses of someone to call a Congressman and tell him to do something about prayers in school? Nope.

Then just what *was* this money to be used for? For parties, dinners, and travel expenses of the delegates to the district and national PTA meetings.

You think I'm joking, don't you? No, I'm not; really! Well, there were a few other things, like five dollars for a police lieutenant to come to one of the meetings and discuss drug use and abuse. Oh yes, I almost forgot—thirty-five dollars for gifts for the room that had the most parents attending PTA and five dollars for the library. The room mothers didn't even get any money for buying those hard cookies that no one likes to eat at PTA meetings.

I'll just have to digress here for a moment and tell you what I saw the other day in a first-grade classroom. Talk about kicking out teachers! I wanted to kick this one in just the right place. It wasn't the first time I had seen this kind of thing, and I'm sorely afraid it won't be the last time. This was one of those rooms in which the teacher was a great believer in using charts to show the "progress" of the kids in her class. There was a spelling chart with its gold stars and blank spaces; a reading chart showing the number of books each child had or had not read; and there was a penmanship chart showing the progress made by the children in that skill. And then there was one labeled in big letters: OUR MOMS AND DADS GO TO PTA. The names of the kids were listed, and beside each child's name was a series of gold stars and/or blackened spaces indicating that one or both parents had or had not attended PTA meetings.

I had to laugh outright even though it was as sad as it was funny. How much control does a first-grader have over his parents' attendance at PTA? Ah, the wisdom of some of our tenured teachers. Sometimes we teachers become great peanut peddlers.

Back to that PTA budget that I was talking about. On one occasion I questioned the president of the PTA about it, copies of which were being distributed just as she was calling for a vote of approval on it. You see, exactly three-fourths of that budget was to be used for the Christmas party, a dinner for the teachers at which we parents were to express our appreciation to them and for them, the end-of-the-year party for the sixth grade, trip-expense money to the conventions, etc. So I asked about it. I shouldn't have. Do you know what the president replied? (Of course you don't; you weren't there!) She said: "Well, don't you believe in letting the children have fun?"

I told her I was in favor of God, the country, and mother. And children, too. But I didn't know, I said, that the main goal of the PTA was to show children a good time. She asked me if I would like to attend the next executive council meeting of the PTA, almost daring me to say yes. I said yes. She didn't invite me, even though I assured her that I was not afraid of the executive council. But it seems that the principal was going to be out of town for a few days, and the next meeting would not be held until he returned. Apparently he never did return, because she never did invite me to the next one—or the next!

But the budget emphasis did change the next year somewhat. There weren't as many parties, anyway. But it did not include anything about prayer or Bible-reading or God. All of these had been successfully excluded from the classroom and we have accepted another religion now. It is being industriously taught in the schools but it is not called religion. It is called atheism, but not out loud. Atheism, you see, is just another form of religion.

The most pitiful and laughable incongruity of all time exists in our now Godless classrooms. Get this: The only time we are allowed to mention God in school is when we are teaching *against* Him. Or (and now the ut-utmost) when we are using His name as an *expletive* or *epithet*. This, ladies and gentlemen (and teachers) is true atheism.

At a recent meeting of the American Association of Colleges for Teacher Education one of the speakers told us he was not allowed to talk about religion. Nor did he, but throughout his speech he interjected the name of the Deity several times as part of his epithetic vocabulary. This appeared acceptable to the audience, as it applauded from time to time and laughed appreciatively at his would-be wit. Had he been giving a favorable word to God, or of God, I suppose the audience would have been afraid to applaud for fear of being thought too religiously inclined. But I don't know.

Comes the science class and how the earth came to be. What happens? The science books and the teachers talk about the "bang" theory. You know, the one about the big explosion taking place somewhere, some time, out in space, and one of the pieces wandering off and becoming Earth. Then there's the part-of-the-sun theory, i.e., the earth was formerly a part of the sun, etc.

These theories abound. But the only definite word we have on the subject, the Bible, the teacher is supposed to gloss over, even to the point of pooh-poohing it. Admittedly, the whole story of the Creation is not there, but *a* story is and it's the *only* one we have. But we can't use it because it has the word "God" in it, and this makes it unscientific. This we have to tell the pupils, so we can't use it. And we can't tell them the Genesis story of the creation of man because that isn't scientific either, and it also mentions God as the main character. So out that story goes. If we tell them that man came from seaweed, we're on safe ground as far as the religionist atheists are concerned. If we teach the kids that their ancestors were low-browed beasts, we're still ok. Indeed, we can teach them just about anything we wish about the origin of man and get by with it, as long as we leave God out of the picture. Our atheist friends have seen to that, and we are swallowing it. Or they want us to swallow it, thus accepting their religion.

So we tell the kids, finally, that we don't know how the earth and man came into existence, but we know it wasn't the way it says it was in the only story we have about it. Then some smart-aleck kid asks how we know that it *didn't* come about that way. Well, we say somewhat indignantly and in a withering tone of voice, Darwin, who was in the real know, and some others who got to be in the know also, told us so. And anyway, that other story talks about God and we're not supposed to talk about Him any more. It's grossly unscientific, too.

Now, while we can't talk about God existing (even long enough to make the earth and man), we *can* talk about Him *not* existing. That is, we can tell the kids about "Water-puppy Day." You mean you haven't heard about Water-puppy Day? Well, that was the day (assuming that there *were* days at the time!) 39½ million or trillion years ago, when a water-puppy flopped out of his watery home onto dry ground, and liked it so much he decided to stay and become our ancestor. We don't know when that happened, how it happened, or even if it *did* happen, but as long as we say that it happened in prehistoric times, and that God had nothing to do with it, we can guess and lie about it to the kids all we wish.

Blooey. And phooey, too.

But you just try to stop this kind of thing and see where you wind up. The Darwins and the Scopeses and the O'Haras will see you in court. Yeah. Because they have definite proof about things like the water-puppy and other adventure stories. By the way, someone has suggested, facetiously or otherwise, that with all of the celebrating of famous people's birthdays and other anniversaries, we should celebrate Water-puppy Day. Maybe so; we seem to be in the mood for any kind of damn foolishness. They have proof, for example, that horses can twitch their muscles to scare off bothersome flies. Point one. They also have proof that most humans can raise their eyebrows and wrinkle their foreheads. Point two. Therefore, about 39½ million or trillion years ago horses were people and people were horses. That is, they (we?) were of the same "stock." Point zero.

Hey, don't hit me! I didn't start that rumor. My old friend Charles Darwin did. (Don't forget, you heard it first from Charley!) But it has been picked up and confirmed by my Godless friends, and now that's the kind of religion they are advocating. And that's the only kind of religion we're allowed to teach in the public schools. The PTA buys it because the school administration buys it. And we, the people, buy it because we are afraid to do otherwise. We want to appear sophisticated and learned. We certainly can't if we accept that stuff that's in the Bible, can we? And we don't want to oppose the schools. They know best how and what to teach our kids. We know this is true because the school people have told us so. So there!

It reminds me of the seventh-grade teacher who told her students, "Whatever religion you claim to have is the right religion and it's the wrong religion. No one knows which one is correct, or whether there is a God. The people who worship the sea as their God might be just as right as any of you who claim to worship another thing as your God. The people who believe that our original ancestor was seaweed might be right. Who knows? We just don't know where we came from, or how things got started." This is the kind of *no religion* that is being taught in school, at least by some teachers. And when one of the kids asked about that story in the Bible, this teacher replied that it was just that, i.e., a story only, which intelligent people cannot believe and which science has disproved. Then she added, "And I am not supposed to discuss religion nor God in school." Then when that same student asked her why she was doing it, she answered that she felt it was her duty to clear up this "nonsense about the Bible and God."

Now do you begin to see what I mean? This is not an isolated case. I've heard this kind of thing repeated again and again in the classroom. Again, while we are not allowed to teach about God and the Bible in the public schools, we are allowed to teach that there is *not* such a Being, and that the Bible has been declared passé. Again, whose *no religion* are we talking about? It is apparent that we are given full sway to teach no-religion and no-God, but that we can't teach belief *in* one. Now that's more than passin' strange, I say. What are we coming to?

But it's even more than that. Our college professors of religion are the leaders often in this drive to oust God from the classroom. Not long ago a college junior came to my office crying. She said she had just come from a religion class where the professor had spent the entire period proving in a highly deriding manner that the Bible is "just a collection of sweet stories." She said that he had derided and laid low all the things concerning religion which she had been taught as a child, and that it was extremely upsetting to her. She said that she had no desire to return to that class, but that it was a required course which she had to take in order to graduate. What could or should she do? She said to me, "I believe in God, I always have. Now my professor of *Christianity* tells me there *is* no God, and that the Bible is nothing. And this man is sometimes asked to fill the pulpit in my church on Sundays. What am I supposed to do?"

Frankly, I didn't know what to tell the girl, except to stand up in class and tell the professor to go to the hell in which he did not believe.

Of course this was a college class, and in college, we are allowed to teach almost anything we want, up to a point. Often the college administration is afraid to interfere for fear of being accused of denying a professor his academic freedom. So it is doubtful that the administration would have done anything about this situation which the girl described. I knew this, of course, and anyway, one professor does not go tattle on another. You see, he might have gone and tattled on me because I was teaching just the opposite, i.e., that there *is* a God, and that, simple and naïve as it makes me appear, I believe the Bible. I am not a religion professor. I teach in the field of education, but the subject of the teaching of religion often comes up in my classes because I work with people who are going to be teaching youngsters. And, if in the religion classes they can teach no-religion, then surely in an education class I should be able to teach *some* religion. If in a religion class there can be taught no-God, then I should be able to teach in my class some-God. That seems fair to me, anyway. Democratic, equal rights, etc. Right?

Pursuing further the acceptance of the Godless classroom, let me give further illustration of what we have come to accept as a Godless-religion form of teaching in the public schools. In one of my daughter's classrooms in high school there was a discussion of ancient gods of the Greeks and the Romans. During the discussion the history teacher, being full of knowledge and baloney, made this statement: "As far as I know, God might be a southern, black, Jewish negress." Now, I submit, ladies and gentlemen, that had he stated that he knew God to be that which is generally taught in a Sunday School class in a Christian church, he would have been hailed into the principal's office for teaching religion. But as long as he was speaking *against* God, he was on safe ground. You can't be fired for teaching no-God, or no-religion. You can't be fired for using His name as an expletive; but just don't try teaching a positive God. That's against the rules.

Not only is it against the rules, but one puts oneself in danger of being thought simple, naïve, unscientific, and unsophisticated. This was the essence of the conversation at a luncheon table recently where a renowned professor of chemistry had finally yielded the floor (table) to someone else to speak. He had been discussing the age of the earth, the age of man, etc., when someone broke in with the thought that "and then there's the Bible." Roars of laughter. Ha, ha, they all said, except the one who had made the unlearned remark. The chemistry man, during the ensuing conversation, pointed out to his more unlearned colleague, that bringing the Bible into any discussion concerning the how's, when's and who's of the earth's age and formation, was stupid. And he said, "This is truly a matter for science to settle, not religion. It has to be taken care of in a scientific manner," he declared. He ended his rather vigorous remarks by stating that he hoped that his colleague would have sense enough *not* to bring God and the Bible into his classroom lectures.

But my unscientific friend embarrassed the scientific chemist. He made mention of the unmasking of Mr. Piltdown, that well-known ancestor of ours that turned out not to be an ancestor after all. Mr. Piltdown, you recall, had his picture in our scientific books for forty years. Every school kid learned about him and was given a low grade if he didn't find out about him, and this went on for nearly a half century. He was one of those "proofs" of no-God making man. My unscientific friend had the audacity to point out that in this particular instance science had fallen on its face. (Hold on now; I'm not against science. I'd vote for it any day. I'm in favor of it but I'd vote against the Piltdown man and the water-puppy as being our first ancestors, especially when these are substituted with great favor as part of the teaching in our public schools. I am against this kind of no-God, no-religion teaching in the schools, when at the same time some-God and some-religion are illegal.)

The whole point here is that we have thrown out God and religion from our schools, and made them illegal. At the same time, we have bought, "whole hog" it seems, the atheistic form of belief, which is another form of religion, and have made it legal to teach it in our public schools. In short, we have made it illegal to teach one form of religion, and have made it legal to teach another form. Blooey and phooey again!

Let me show you further what I mean. My ten-year-old daughter came home from school the other day and announced that she had to give a talk on "prejudice" the next day. According to her, the talk was to be concerned with the Negroes and the whites, and their treatment of each other. We explained to her that prejudice may take many forms, and that this was just one of them. She said her teacher told them that it was *not* to be about God or religion and prejudice, because we really don't know whether there is a God. "And we don't talk about God in school," my daughter said the teacher said. That teacher does not talk about God in public school except to say that there is probably not one. Again we find that crazy and disturbing factor about the public schools and God: We can teach that He is dead or that He never existed, but we are not allowed to say that He might now exist. I would hate to have to justify this kind of thinking to someone who happens to ask about it.

But if we think that the above situation is out of this world, just listen to this next foul stupidity on our part. Truly the width and depth of erroneous thought has not yet reached its ultimate. To reiterate or restate a position, we are not allowed to teach God, religion, or prayer in the public school classroom. It is said that it is unconstitutional to do so, and that public tax money cannot and must not be used to support religion and its various components in this manner. I find no quarrel with this. The church and state must be kept separate. The quarrel, I believe, comes when we institute a new kind of religion, the no-religion and no-God. But then we reverse ourselves completely and present before our public the most horrible and inexcusable of all incongruities. *We have about decided now that it is our duty to pay various groups to teach their religious ideas to anyone who will enter their institutions.* Note that abominable doctrine: We're now going to give public tax money to nonpublic schools where a *particular* form of religion is taught.

What? Use tax money for private purposes? Yes, indeed. Well, you say, how can that be? We can't have prayer in public schools because that would be a misuse of funds, but we can give public funds to private schools for the same purpose? What crazy-headed thinking is this? It's one of those things that a college president recently referred to when he remarked, "The people in this state will fall for any damn-fool idea that comes along."

Such an idea has certainly come along in many states and many school districts. In the State of Illinois right now, for example, the legislature is seriously considering making it legal to pay $30 million of tax money to private schools. Private schools, mind you, where the teaching of God, religion, and prayer is a ritual every day of the school year. But in our regularly tax-supported institutions we aren't even allowed to offer up a prayer or mention the name of the Deity.

It is one of the most idiotic, foolish, and erroneous ideas I have ever heard of. My limited vocabulary disallows me to heap vituperations of sufficient quantity and quality upon those who propose and support such a nefarious project. Call me bigoted, narrow-minded, selfish, and stupid. Yes, I am all of those things, and more. I find myself unable to recognize anything but idiocy in such a proposal; not because I want to see private schools go out of business and close down, and not because I want to see millions of schoolchildren denied the right to attend schools of their choice. But if we are going to spend my money in this manner, I believe we should be fair and allow the same rights and privileges to all children in matters of prayer, religion, and God.

I am quite aware that it would be difficult to please everybody if we were to countenance all kinds of prayers, offerings, etc. Chaos would reign for sure, but justice and good sense are always in order if a teacher will use some, and with the support of the school. The most important thing of all (if we are going to give public funds for private school support) is not to leave the public school classroom *Godless*. Truly, I am not advocating the teaching of any religion in our public schools. The church and the state must be kept separate, but I stand foursquare for God in the public school classroom, and where feasible and in order, the story of the Creation as recorded in the Bible. As an amateur historian, this story makes more sense than the water-puppy story, or the seaweed story, or the ape-human story. It also makes as much sense as the "'bang" theory of the creation of the earth, or any one of the hundreds of ideas about how everything living came into being or existence. Anything prehistoric must be purely (?) postulated hypotheses. If it were otherwise, it would not be prehistoric; it would be historic. That's good logic, isn't it? And let it be remembered that a hypothesis is only a high-class term for guess.

The PTA, bless its weak-kneed little heart, will stand by, not idly of course, while foes are tearing at our grass roots. But as I just said, it will not be idle. No, indeed! The telephone lines are kept hot by the vigorous workers lining up room mothers, arranging for chile and beans suppers, cookies for PTA meeting night, and the *big event* of the year, "THE HALLOWEEN CARNIVAL!"

Chapter IX

Kindling Hope
for Kindergarten Kids

or Oh, Oh, Look, Look, See Dick and Jane Read Fast

It makes me *so mad* when I hear people, teachers and parents alike, say that "You have to teach a child to read before he can read fast." This is just another example of the abysmal ignorance under which we are continuing to suffer when it comes to discussing the learning processes. Of course, the reason this kind of comment is made is that we have been in the bad habit of making kids wait until they have reached first grade before we let them begin to read. We've always done it that way, so that's the best way, it seems. More lousy and lazy thinking. And some of the most knowledgeable reading "experts" maintain that we should wait until a child has reached junior high school before we introduce any concepts of increased rate of reading or spelling or "mathing." Indeed, much of the fault of our sorry reading situation today must be laid at the feet of these experts. They are the ones who write the books and have made the poor teachers believe the lies they tell in those books.

You ought to see that group of thirteen kindergarteners over there in that small town in northeast Missouri! And their teacher. She has been teaching for a long time but she must have missed some of those books on reading which say that we're not supposed to teach kindergarten kids to read. I'm glad she missed them. If she had read them, she might be like most other kindergarten and first-grade teachers; she might have believed their piddling pronouncments about not teaching young children to read. Even as I write this, that old feeling of frustration comes over me as I realize again the abominable things with which they have saddled us.

116

This damnable doctrine becomes even worse when we consider what pediatricians, psychologists, and others tell us about the treatment of babies. They tell us to begin training the baby from the time he is born to see, to hear, to respond in various ways. They tell us that it's those first three or four years that are really the significant ones in a person's life. This is when the real learning takes place, they say, learning that is lasting and of great significance to the child as an individual. Yet we wait until a child is five or six years old before we start his formal training in school. Doesn't make sense, does it?

And even after we start him in kindergarten we prohibit him from reading, but put him through a great many "readiness" tricks which have proved to be pretty useless, considering the number of reading failures we produce. I wonder when we're going to wake up to these facts and demand something really tremendous from our schools and our teachers? Never will I forget the "bawling out" a teacher gave a parent who had taught her child to read before the child entered first grade. That teacher told the mother of the child that "I just hope you have not ruined Mavis for first-grade reading." Well, evidently she hadn't, because the child forged ahead in the first grade in spite of being bored to tears from time to time. Another teacher told a group of parents at PTA meeting one night to "Wait until your child starts school to teach him to read and let someone who is trained to do it teach him." Good grief! There's just no limit to the amount of nonsense, is there?

Remember the story of the mother who asked a famous educator when she should start educating her child? He said to her: "When do you expect your child to be born?" "Born," she exclaimed, "why he's five years old already!" "For goodness sakes, madam," he replied, "run home and start educating him right now. You're five years too late."

And so it goes throughout much of the literature concerning the training and rearing of the young child: Give him lots of experiences of many kinds from the cradle or crib on. Help him to learn as much as possible while his brain is still in the forming or developing stages. Give him room in which to move about, to touch, to feel, to see, to hear. A thousand things we want him to know about, so that by the time he is three or four years of age, he has learned a whole language right from scratch. He can speak in sentences; he can turn the subject and verb around and ask questions; he can speak in long sentences and in short sentences; he can reason, laugh at funny things, enjoy funny movies, etc.

Then he enters school and begins to lose in many respects. Recall again the words of the man on the National Council for Disadvantaged Children: "Every child who enters school becomes disadvantaged." Perhaps this can be pointed up by using the story of the two little first-grade boys during a recess period. A low-flying jet plane went over and the boys, watching it, were discussing the length of the wing span, the number of tons of thrust and the possible number of members of the crew. Just then the bell rang signaling the end of recess. "Oh, oh," said one of the boys, "back to those damn beads again." There are innumerable cases of children bored with the foolishness of many kindergartens, and who are being held back (damned) in first grade because they have to proceed at the rate of the average.

Why is it this way? Tradition and stupidity. Tradition is a terrible thing sometimes. It often shapes our lives, and too often even determines our life's work or outcome. We start children to read when they are six years of age, or in the first grade. We have been doing so for more than a hundred years. This is reason enough to continue, according to many educators. The assumption is that we have been doing something like this for a hundred years; it must be because it has proved to be a good thing. Well, if it *is* good we should continue it; if it isn't, we should change it. Once I wrote a letter to the superintendent of a fairly large city school system, telling him that I thought his teachers were using horse-and-buggy methods in a jet age. I was referring to the obvious philosophy prevailing there about the teaching of reading in the kindergarten and first grade. There was no such thing as reading in the kindergartens in his schools, and the first grades were divided into groups, etc. He replied to my accusation saying that his school system was considered one of the best in the state, and that this was the way they had been doing it for years, and that this was the way they would continue as long as he was superintendent.

You see, it didn't matter that what he was having his kindergarten and first-grade teachers doing was not working. The records of the schools all over the nation were sad proof of that. But what they were doing was good enough, he said. He was satisfied. It was in his school system that a principal of some twenty years of administrating was heard to say that he wanted no innovations in his school. And, as far as I know and have been able to see, he has kept his word. The kindergarten and first-grade teachers are still as limited as ever, and the kids are suffering just as always.

Now I agree that we should not try to teach children to read while they are in kindergarten, and that we should wait until a child has reached the age of six to start him in a reading program, *but only because that is the way those two grades are presently structured.* Maybe I should say because of the *mis*-structuring of those two grades. The child of six is expected to fit into the structure of his first year in school, whether it be kindergarten or first grade (or sixth or seventh, etc.). Far too seldom is the work adjusted to fit him or his needs. We establish certain standards and expect every child to meet those standards. If he doesn't meet them we say that he is too immature, or that he is a slow learner, or a late bloomer, etc. I'm all for setting up certain kinds of standards, but we have to be very careful for *whom* we are setting them, and *why*. The standards may be very worthwhile, but the *methods* used to bring the pupils up to the standards might be blastedly stupid.

That kindergarten teacher in that small town in Missouri who is teaching her kids to read rapidly has set no standards. She wants them all to read and to read fast, but she refuses to standardize the *way* they read, the materials they use, and when they should complete the books and workbooks. And she and those kids are having more fun than any kindergarten group in this whole country. It's a real pleasure to watch them operate. Come and see.

Also, a first-grade teacher in another small town in Missouri is having a wonderful time, except that she can't keep the kids in books. Both she and that kindergarten teacher are hard put to get enough books for the children. You see, their school children are reading from three hundred to two thousand words a minute, and are loving every minute of it. Standards be darned. Standardized methods, too. And workbooks, too.

It is well known that children of the same chronological ages do not necessarily have the same abilities. Some adjustments are attempted in the first grade and other grades by placing the pupils in groups. Sometimes there are only two groups, and sometimes there are four and occasionally there are five. Three, however, is the magical number of groups in the first grade. They are often arranged this way as a result of the "readiness" tests which have been given a few months ago in kindergarten. The same general procedure is used with each group in the teaching-to-read process. Certainly there are some variations in the materials and in the speed at which one group progresses compared with another, but each group receives much the same approach. The pupils within a given group receive, for the most part, the same kind of instruction. Now, this has not proved highly successful, but, as that school superintendent said, "It's the way we've been doing it and we're clinging tenaciously to it." And as a result, the entire nation is in a dither about our terrible reading situation. And well it should be.

I have tried to emphasize throughout this material the need for individualizing reading instruction. When this is done and each child is encouraged to progress as fast as he can, remarkable things begin to take place. Let me illustrate again.

Another first-grade teacher, having received training and experience in rapid reading, decided to experiment with her first-grade children. Because of the rules of the school which required her to maintain three groups in reading, she devoted some time each day to the "regular" methods of teaching. But then, as each child finished his work, she would encourage him to move his eyes faster over the pages. She would also show him different ways of seeing the words, or following a different pattern of eye movement as he read. Again, in keeping with the "regular" method, each child was tested from the level of reader that his group was using.

Because of the usual stupid restrictions placed upon her and the other teachers in the school, it was possible for her to give instruction in rapid reading only occasionally. In fact, when the principal walked in on her one day (principals have a knack for being where they're not wanted) and caught her teaching those kids to have fun in reading, he commanded her to "Leave your stopwatch at home and teach according to the Guidebook." (That blasted Guidebook again!) So it was that she was able to instruct individually only from time to time and even then had to do it sneakily.

But the "damage" had already been done. The principal caught her too late. The children had already caught the vision of greater freedom in reading and some were unhappy when they had to read in the regular group situations. The instructions the teacher had given were simple; the same ones that kindergarten teacher gave her class of thirteen youngsters: "Make your eyes go faster, and see the words straight down the page, or back and forth, or sideways, or even upside down."

What! Upside down? Of course, my dear friend. Many of us see to read upside down quite easily. But unless we can read *better,* as some people can in that manner, there is no point in doing it. By the way, it does not hurt us to do that. It doesn't make us go crazy, either.

There were more instructions (these will be given in more detail later), but most of them were repetitions of the beginning ones. Some of the youngsters preferred to continue using the usual left-to-right movement, and others used modifications of this method. But each was allowed to hold his book in any manner he wished; each was allowed to "slouch" over his desk if he wished, or even to stand up when he read. The only limitations placed on them was that they had to use books that had as few pictures as possible, because books that have a lot of pictures in them necessitate too much page-turning.

Whoa, now. That teacher was not yet having the kids fool around with vocabulary. Remember, in Chapter II I said that we start everybody off with *no comprehension*. That is, we don't care whether they know one word from another. In fact, we'd just as soon they *didn't* know the words. And so it was with the kindergarteners and the first-graders. They weren't supposed to be trying to understand what they were seeing.

Now back to that first-grade teacher who was having to sneak in some good reading for the kids: The children in the highest reading group made the fastest progress, which was to be expected, I suppose. And they were more imaginative in their ways of reading, in moving their eyes over the pages, and in holding their books in different positions. It was extremely interesting to note, however, that some of the children in the two lower groups showed and did some remarkable things.

One seven-year-old boy who was spending his second year in the first grade (and that's a lot of nonsense, too), was severely mixed in hand-foot-eye dominance. He apparently preferred to use his left hand, but told his teacher that his mother slapped his hand when he did this. (It turned out later that his mother was from a foreign country where it was considered a thing of evil for a person to use his left hand.) A conference with the mother resulted in the boy being allowed to use his left hand in writing and in other skill activities. As the weeks went by and he became more adept at using his left side, his word recognition increased as did his speed. When the children were given their "final" test he scored 75 percent on comprehension with a reading speed of 352 words a minute. (Remember that the average silent reading rate for first-graders is 45 to 50 words a minute.) Others in the lower groups made progress; some were outstanding, some showed little or no progress that could be attributed to the different teaching methods. However, these children (there were only a few of them) had some severe learning problems which were being treated by a psychologist.

Again, it should be kept in mind that in all of this, the teacher had to keep what she was doing "under wraps." The principal was "agin" it. The Sacred Guidebook didn't say the teacher was supposed to do this kind of thing. She really had to watch her step. But how could any teacher with a bit of sense and much enthusiasm about her work *keep* from exploiting the kids' minds? Especially when the kids were thoroughly enjoying this kind of learning!

In April of that year the teacher enlisted the cooperation of the other two first-grade teachers in the school in testing all of the children in the three sections of that grade. It was decided to call the first teacher's class the "A" group, and the other two classes the "B" and "C" groups. Only those youngsters in sections B and C had been given the traditional or "regular" type of instruction. But it should be remembered that those pupils in A had received special instruction only on an irregular basis. According to the teacher, they had received no more than a few weeks of training in rapid reading over a seven-month period.

I want you to pay close attention to this next part now, because the testing was carried on so that there could be no question about the authenticity of it. The teacher of section A wanted to be sure that everything was done "scientifically." The children were tested one at a time, with those in the lowest groups in each section taking the same test; all of those in the middle groups in each section taking a separate test designed for them; and those in the highest group being administered a test from the books they had been using, but from selections which they had not read previously.

It should be noted that, according to the school policy, all of the children in the highest groups in the first grade had to use the same books, those in the next groups used another set of of readers throughout the grade, while the children in the lowest groups used a third set of readers. It was from these books that the children were tested, each child reading from the same book as all other children in his group. None of the children had been tested "officially" before the experiment began because it was just an idea the teacher of section A had had to help the youngsters. In the words of the teacher, "It had started just as a lark, really, then I began to get serious about it as we progressed."

The results of the testing were downright startling. The

class which had received some training in speed techniques far outstripped the other two sections which had been taught the way most first grades are taught. In both rate and comprehension, section A was far out ahead of the other two traditional grades. All three of the classes involved in the testing were supposedly "average" first-grade classes. The pupils had been placed in the various sections in no particular order except to make sure that each teacher had about the same number of fast, medium, and slow youngsters in her section.

READING SCORES (RATE AND COMPREHENSION)
OF THREE FIRST-GRADE CLASSES

	Sec. A	Sec. B	Sec. C
Average percent of Comprehension	86	76	73
Average number of words per minute	512	69	75
Highest Individual Comp.	90	100	90
Lowest Individual Comp.	20	10	10
Highest Individual Speed	1512	235	267
Lowest Individual Rate	78	30	25

You can read the table above for yourselves, but let me point out some significant differences. And as you read these figures, can you honestly say that the way we usually teach reading to little kids is the best way? Note, please, that the group which had received even the small amount of instruction in faster reading read more than five times as fast as the two groups which had been taught the way the Guidebook says to teach. Furthermore, the average comprehension of the "speed" class, was 1,512 words per minute with 86 percent comprehension. Compare, please. The highest speed attained by a pupil in the other two groups was 267 wpm with 100 percent comprehension.

Another interesting comparison of these results can be made by obtaining a Reading Efficiency Index (REI). This is done by multiplying the rate of words read per minute by the percent of comprehension and dividing the product by 100.

Using this formula, the average REI of Group A above would be 440.32. The average REI of Groups B and C would be 53.59. This would mean a difference of 386.73 in Reading Efficiency!

Using the formula on an individual basis, i.e., taking the highest individual pupil's scores from each of the three groups, we find mighty interesting results. The Reading Efficiency Index of the highest pupil in Group A was 1125, and that in Group B was 267, while the highest in Group C was 212. And notice the tremendous difference between the highest of the first group and the lowest of Group C.

As I look at these results I again find myself flying into a purple rage. What damnably stupid things we do to the kids in school! Only last night my first-grade daughter sat in a class with some older students who were learning to read rapidly. She was there only because she had requested to be allowed to go. She was the slowest reader in that class, only reading around five hundred words a minute, but with fine understanding, but then she was not a regular attender of the class. A boy of high school age was talking with her after the class about her reading there and in school. She told him that she doesn't read that way in school, because she is not supposed to do so. Then she said, "Sometimes it's not very much fun to read in school because I have to wait until everybody is through reading a story before I can go on. That's why I wanted to come to daddy's class tonight, so I could have fun."

I felt like crying when I heard her say that.

We conducted a reading program in North Carolina with twenty-five children in the first grade. They showed a definite increase in both speed and comprehension after nine weeks of instruction given on a daily basis. The periods were thirty minutes in length. The average reading rate of the twenty-five youngsters was thirty-six words a minute before the program began. I must tell you though, and this is significant, that this study was a part of a "poverty program" and these children came from deprived areas and homes. The average comprehension of this group in the beginning was 51 percent.

At the end of the nine weeks these children read at an average rate of 503 words per minute with 74 percent comprehension. The highest single rate of speed was 905 words a minute with a comprehension score of 98 percent! The lowest reading rate on the last examination was 75 words per minute with 63 percent comprehension.

Should I tell you what the average I.Q. score was of that group? At the risk of being called a liar, I'll have to tell you. According to the school records it was 77. What are you reading experts going to do about that? Well, wait a minute. If you will read the last chapter of this book, you will find this kind of situation elaborated upon, and perhaps find it quite interesting.

Now, *how,* brown cow? How do we teach them?

First, the school (administrators and teachers) must have caught the vision of the greater learning possibilities of the children. This is a must. The teachers must *not* be like that first-grade teacher who said, "Individualized reading doesn't work. I tried it one afternoon and it didn't work at all." They must be dedicated to the proposition that every child can learn far beyond what we have previously decreed for him. They have to throw out some old ideas and methods, and remember that no two children learn exactly the same way, nor do they need to learn exactly the same thing at the same time.

If they are to adequately instruct the children, they themselves must have some exercise in rapid reading. The kindergarten teacher of that class in Missouri learned the principles of rapid learning, then began to pass them on to her youngsters. The children responded even quicker than did she to what was being taught, and this is the way it usually works. There must also be on hand plenty of easy books. It is difficult to find such books with few pictures, but get as many as possible. Books with mostly pictures must be avoided. A child can spend literally half his reading time just turning pages, and there is not much learned in that activity as such. That kindergarten teacher told me recently that her big problem now is keeping the kids in reading materials. They have just about exhausted their supply of books, she said.

The children must be taught from the beginning to see the words rapidly, paying no attention to what the words say. *No comprehension,* remember. You are getting them in the habit of seeing rapidly, of moving their eyes over the pages fast. Most kindergarten children have not been taught to read before entering school, so it will be easier to teach them than some others. They should be instructed to see words rapidly from left to right at first, because this is the direction in which they will write. Later, after learning the left-to-right concept, they should be encouraged to increase the ways of seeing the words, i.e., straight down or straight up a page, spiraling from right to left, or from left to right zigzagging down and/or up, etc. But for the beginning instruction, the left-to-right concept should be employed.

At the outset a few of the children will already know some of the words they are seeing. Most of them will not know any of them. But again, for this part of the program, it matters little whether they know the words or do not know them. They must be shown how to move their eyes rapidly across the page, recognizing the words only as blocks of print. Some of the children will have to be told several times that the letters between the spaces are *words,* and that they are to see those letters or blocks of print as rapidly as they would watch a speeding car or airplane moving along its route. The teacher may wish to make a game of this activity and say to the youngsters: "Let's see who can get to the bottom of the page first. Play like you are an airplane and *fly* as fast as you can, but be sure you see every word. Here, I'll show you how."

You then demonstrate, moving your finger under the lines smoothly in a left-to-right direction. As you do this you emphasize the smoothness of the movement. You tell the kids to stop or to slow down only when there is a road mark (period, comma, etc.), then go right on again as fast as they can go. You see, smoothness in seeing is one of the problems with kids and adults who don't read well. In the primary grades they are actually taught to see slowly and in a stumbling manner, to pause to figure out a word, to repeat, etc. It's a practice that surely must have been designed by the devil himself to keep us from learning to read well. So smoothness is one of the things we work for right from the beginning.

Some of the children will be unable to follow the lines with their eyes only, and the teacher should encourage them to use their fingers as she had been doing. Now don't get horrified at the thought of using the finger for pointing. I know that it's tabooed by many of the writers of the reading textbooks, but so what? They just don't know what they are talking about. If it helps a child to follow the lines, and at the same time gives him a sense of comfort or security, and helps to guide his eyes, why not have him do it? It helps many of them. Try it. It's even good for many adults.

You, or whoever is doing the teaching, must move about among the children to ascertain which of them need special help and attention. It is to be expected that each child will perform in a manner different from every other one. The teacher's job here is to make sure that each pupil performs in the way that is best suited for him. This includes the way(s) a child wants to hold his book. Remember that we do not all see best from the same angle, and that some people (children and adults) can see better when their reading materials are placed in a different position from the ones that you and I are in the habit of using. So if a child wants to hold his book sideways, let him, if that proves to be a good position for him from which to see.

Some of the youngsters will be able to go much faster than others, while a few will have difficulty moving their eyes from one end of the line to the other. Again, it is this smoothness in reading that is one of the important things for which we are working, so careful attention is to be given each child to make sure that he develops this ability. I must repeat this, that one of the problems with which the kindergarten and primary grade teachers constantly contend is that slow, stumbling, tedious, stuttering-type reading which many children exhibit. And unless it's corrected early it will stay with them throughout their lives. But blast it! It's the teachers who encourage them with it, aided and abetted by those better-to-never-have-been-written guidebooks and workbooks. I wish we could have a big book-burning party, with those books contributing the major flames.

I must point out again that it is important at this stage that no effort be made on the part of the teacher to have the children attempt to recognize the words. The important thing is to encourage them to see words quickly, smoothly, and as many as possible at a time, going from left to right, until the habit is securely fixed. Now, I know that this is contrary to what is generally taught and contrary to the way most of us learned to read. However, most of us have been taught poorly, and most of us learned to read poorly. No one can deny that, for sure. The time allowed for this kind of practice will vary with each child, and it is the teacher's responsibility to determine when a child is ready to begin word recognition activities.

As the "seeing" activities progress, interesting variations in the children may be observed. Some of them will find that moving their eyes across each line, one line at a time, will slow them down. Then they, with the help and encouragement of the teacher, might find that they can see the words better and faster if they move their eyes in a zigzag fashion down the page. A few of them will be able to go straight down the left-hand page and straight up the right-hand side, or in a number of other ways.

Extreme care must be taken in this matter to see that each is progressing as he is best able. Children of this age are inclined to follow the lead of those around them, and some are likely to copy the action of others who are succeeding nicely, in order to "save face." It is up to the teacher to guard against this and see to it that each pupil experiments with different methods of seeing the words until he finds the best way or ways of seeing them for himself in a rapid and smooth manner. This should be a "fun time" for the teacher and the children. She must move around the room to listen, demonstrate, test, and suggest. This has to be done several times during each "seeing" session. The fun is in watching the peculiar and interesting things the children do as they learn the concept of moving their eyes rapidly "like an airplane flies."

In addition to developing the habit of going smoothly in

reading, it aids in broadening one's span of vision in all directions. We have found that many five- and six-year-olds, after a few hours of this kind of practice, are able to see several lines at a time, while still others see only one line or a few words. But invariably, all develop a faster and smoother way of seeing and reading. Some of those kindergarten kids that I keep talking about seem to look down *between* the pages, with their books partially closed. It's *most* interesting to watch them.

As the children progress in seeing the words rapidly, the teacher begins to teach them some of the words and their meanings. This process may be a little different with each child, depending on many things. His entire background before coming to school, as well as his previous experience in seeing words, will have an effect on his ability to recognize and learn their meaning. It is the teacher's responsibility to determine, as far as possible, each child's peculiar needs and abilities and give the necessary help to each one. For some of the children this will mean drill on word-attack skills. For others it will mean exercises on seeing similarities between words and symbols. She must remember that too much drill can drill a child dead to reading, a thing in which many teachers have become experts. Great care must be taken by the teacher to see that each child receives just what he needs. New speed techniques may be suggested for some of the pupils. Others may need to slow down in their eye movements in order to gain better comprehension.

A few of the youngsters will profit from additional instruction in how to hold their books, i.e., how to slant their books in order to see the words better. A common mistake made by teachers in general in all grades is in assuming that children see the same way in reading. However, we have learned that even as early as kindergarten and first grade there are extreme differences in the angles at which children see most effectively. The teacher then, must be aware of these differences and possibilities, and must be constantly alert to needed changes, and be ready to offer suggestions as needed. It is a part of the individualized process in teaching that every pupil be encouraged to read in the way that brings the best results for him.

In order for this to be accomplished the teacher must observe daily the way the children are performing. She must give aid and direction in "book holding," eye-movement patterns, comprehension techniques, word-attack skills, rates of reading, level of materials, enjoyment from what is being read, and the smoothness in the left-to-right movement of the eyes.

As in any classroom situation, there will be those who require much more attention and guidance than others. It is quite likely, however, that no two pupils will require the same kind of help at the same time. In school in the regular class in reading, all the kids in one group get the same dose, or the same pill. Not so here. Each child is strictly an individual. Reading is strictly an individual affair and should be taught as such. A few of the children may need to continue the left-to-right practice for a longer period, but not at the same rate. Others should be given demonstrations and suggestions on additional eye-movement patterns which they should try for better and more comfortable reading.

One or two of the children, or even more, may find that the "regular" way of turning pages slows them down. After close questioning by the teacher and demonstrations by the pupils, the teacher might suggest and illustrate a faster way of turning the pages by flipping them off the thumb of the right hand. This kind of thing happened just recently in my own experience. I concluded that the two first-grade girls who had complained that their fingers kept slipping on the pages as they tried to turn them rapidly probably had some kind of photographic memory. They seemed to require only a quick glance at the pages in order to absorb the material. This disturbing thought kept recurring to me: If there are two children with this kind of ability in a group of fifteen pupils, how many must there be with similar abilities among the 56 million students in this country? And what are we doing to them by not allowing them to extend and expand their abilities?

Page-turning for these children might continue to be an annoyance to them unless the book or material is bound in such a manner as to allow the pages to flip smoothly, one at a time. If the pages flip by in "clumps" with more than one page going by at a time, the reader wastes time and comprehension in having to go back and separate the "clumps" page by page. (A note here to book publishers: Anyone who reads at a rapid rate can profit considerably more from books which are bound in such a way that the pages turn more smoothly from front to back than from back to front, as the pages in most books do now.)

Again, care must be taken by the teacher to make sure that other children continue in their best way of seeing the words and reading. Some of them, realizing the kind of attention that a few are receiving from their somewhat unusual way of reading and turning pages, might attempt the same kind of thing hoping to convince themselves and the teacher that they can do it, too. It is a natural thing for them to want to do this, and the teacher must quietly and quickly curb the idea by reminding them that she, too, reads best the way *they* are reading. Occasionally, the teacher really has to bear down on a child who insists that he can "read just like Kenny." Kenny is his best friend and there is a strong desire to do or to be like Kenny.

I want it impressed upon all teachers and parents (and you, too, Mr. School Administrator) that in a reading program such as is discussed here, there is no room for group uniformity, despite what the Guidebook says. Unless, of course, it can be definitely shown that such uniformity brings best results. I have indicated previously, and rather loudly, in one way and another, that insistence on uniformity has helped to make of us a nation of poor readers. Let's quit it.

However, this does not mean that there should be no group reading activities. We know that being a part of a group often serves to motivate many children. Thus the teacher will find that she will want to discuss and/or practice with a large or a small group together, sometimes with the entire class, and at other times with only one or two or three children at a time. Occasionally the makeup of the group will be the same two or three days consecutively, while at other times the groups will differ daily. Often there will be no groups at all. Regardless of the group makeup, however, the teacher must remember that the individual's child response is what she must be concerned with, not the total group response.

Does this kind of instruction really bring comprehension as well as speed? Yes, it really does. "But," you say, "how do the children come to know and recognize the words?" Simple. You use a hundred different ways of teaching them, and they see these words hundreds of times in a matter of minutes. In other words, they encounter thousands of words hundreds of times daily. It's the same principle we use in the special classes in foreign languages where we teach the students to read rapidly and, at the same time, to learn to read that language. It's the same principle we use in teaching rapid spelling and math, and the same one we use in teaching people to read rapidly when they already know the language.

In teaching kindergarteners and first-graders who have not yet gone through this process we call learning to read, we also *tell* them what the words are. For example, when we get ready to move into understanding with these youngsters, we use experience charts which the children have made up with our help. We read them aloud, that is the teacher reads it aloud, then has the children read it aloud as the teacher points to each word. Then the teacher says, "Now let's see if we can read it the way we did before you started learning the words. Remember to fly like an airplane, and go fast." She then moves the pointer under the words *rapidly* and *smoothly,* and the children follow along silently. She says, "How many of you know what this word is?" pointing to a certain word. "How about this one?" "And this one?" "Now let's read it again *fast*." Then, "Do you see any words here that you saw in your books as you were looking at the words a while ago?"

Then back to the books. The teacher moves about, checking each child to see what he is doing, giving suggestions here and there, having some of the children looking more closely at some of the words and perhaps having some of them singling out one word that is causing them to stumble or slow down. The whole process is repeated again and again; sometimes with the same story and sometimes with new and different stories. Word comparisons are made and discussed, with some of the children repeating them and others going on to new stories. It is not a hit-and-miss affair. The teacher is keeping track of what each child needs and is pushing each one to go as far as he can. She questions each one about *how* he is seeing the words, *how* he holds his book, and "Is that the best way for you?" she asks. And, "Do you know most of the words, and which ones aren't you sure of?" The questioning and the checking continue. A child doesn't know a word. The teacher asks if he remembers having seen it before in another place. Maybe so, maybe no. They check it together. Maybe for this child the word needs to be syllabicated, or similarities between it and another word pointed out.

I have to point out again that these kids are not the "three-words-a-day" kids. Nor do they encounter them just a few times in a fifteen- or twenty-minute reading period. These youngsters are encountering the words *hundreds,* and maybe even *thousands* of times in fifteen or twenty minutes. They *have* to learn them. It's like the baby who hears thousands of words spoken every day. There is not any way you could keep him from learning to talk if he is anywhere near normal. And these kids learn to read, and read rapidly. Can they do otherwise? Heck no. And they *love* it. They'd almost rather read like this than eat when they're hungry. Yeah, they would. They want to come to school early and stay late, and hurry through noon meal and get back to the room to practice.

The teacher is constantly challenging them. She pushes them to go faster and farther in a shorter period of time. Indeed, if you give them too much time in which to complete a particular assignment they become bored and restless. Like the teacher mentioned before who gave them five minutes to do a page of math problems. Long before the time was up the kids were making airplanes out of their papers and flying them back and forth to each other. Another teacher (I didn't know she would be this dumb) told the kids they would have ten minutes in which to do the assignment. Then she said, "Now I know that this is a heavy assignment [160 math problems and 160 spelling words] and you won't be able to do them all, but please try to do as many as you can." So the kids did only a comparatively few of the math problems and spelling words. There was no challenge. But the next teacher took over and gave them the devil for being so lazy. *She* said to them: "You have fifteen seconds in which to do them all. Now you get them done." They did and had spare time.

I'm convinced that our kids can do *anything* when it comes to brainwork, but we have to give them the opportunity to do so. They love to be exploited when it is done in the right way and when they can see some advantageous results coming from it. There are literally thousands and thousands of teachers who should be charged every day with criminal neglect of our schoolchildren. They deliberately hold back the learning of the kids. Like that idiot of a teacher who told the mother of that child that if the child were to read too fast, she would go crazy. Or like the teacher who would not let the kids learn more than three words a day in reading. And like that principal who threatened to dismiss the student teacher from his school if she allowed a child to read more than one story a day from his book. And the imbecilic remark of the teacher who told a student teacher that the kids could only work on one social studies project at a time. That is, the entire classroom had to be concerned about one project at a time only. She indicated that if they did as suggested, they would finish the book before the end of the year. DTSS—FSA!

Criminal negligence. That's what it is.

Chapter X

How to Hurt the Hurt Kids in School

Those hurt kids are the ones whom we teachers damaged once we got them in what children call "Kids' Prison," meaning school. They were doing fine until *we* got hold of them. Then, *Zowie!*

Take Allen, for example. He was a bit small for his age, so when it came time for him to start kindergarten, the teacher decided that he would stay two years in that grade. Why? Because he looked as though he couldn't cut the mustard. Now, it happened that Allen was a precocious child and had learned to read, write, and do arithmetic before he was five years of age, but in kindergarten he had to play little games, color pictures of ducks and rabbits, and do all kinds of nonsense. You see, the teacher was "getting him ready" to read. Allen was bored with the stuff in school, so bored, in fact, that he became a nuisance and refused to "join in" with the other kids in many of their activities. The teacher pronounced him "immature" and said, "I told you so." She had decided from the day he had entered kindergarten that he would be there with her for two years. So he was.

In the meantime, at home Allen was making some progress. He learned to play checkers and chess and could usually beat his father at the games. He could play circles around his mother. And he could also play the piano; but he didn't like to play with blocks and color rabbits. He became a bit of an outcast at school. He finally got into the first grade, but by this time he was already discouraged. His "readiness" tests showed that he was capable of doing good work, but for some reason, the teacher told his parents, he just was not doing it. Some reason my hind foot! It was that blasted school that was keeping him from progressing. He didn't stand a chance.

136

And so it was that in early October of Allen's sixth-grade year, Allen, who was sitting right near the door of the room, heard his teacher tell the teacher across the hall that "I'm going to flunk Allen this year." You see, Allen could not read the books on a sixth-grade level. Whose fault was that? Why, Allen's, of course. Certainly one could not blame those wise teachers and the principal for what they had done to him those six long years that they had him under their thumb every day.

So when Allen heard the teacher say she was going to flunk him, that broke it: Allen gave up. It was then that his mother came to see me to ask if something could be done to help him. We had some long conferences accompanied by many tears. I felt so sorry for both Allen and his parents as I listened to their story. It was sad indeed. Allen was doing wonderful things at home, but in school he was a flop. He was still small for his age and that made it easier for his teacher to retain him in the sixth grade. It didn't make it easier for Allen, you understand. He was just a little boy, a sort of nonentity in the school. I suppose the school was sure it was doing the right thing for Allen.

I began working with Allen, and one of the first things I asked his parents to do was to take him to a doctor and have him given a thorough physical examination. This they did and the doctor gave him a clean bill of health. But after the doctor had just about finished with his examination, the mother said to the medical man, "Doctor, will you examine his eyes? I wonder if they're all right." I suppose the doctor was a busy man, as most doctors are, and he said to Allen, "Turn around here, boy, and let me see your eyes." Allen turned and looked at the doctor, and the doctor looked straight into Allen's eyes from a distance of about three feet. Then the doctor, having finished his eye examination, declared: "There's nothing wrong with that boy's eyes."

Well. . . .

I'm really not going to make Allen's story a book-length novel. His parents finally took him to an eye doctor and it was found that he was farsighted in one eye and nearsighted in the other. There was so much energy required of him for the "yoking" process that he had little left over for learning. This, coupled with the background methods and philosophy used on him, had caused Allen to drop far behind in school. He had been able to accomplish much at home because of his high interest in some of those activities, and actually excelled in them. But he had little left over for the dull and dry schoolwork which he could not master anyway. All of that tended to work against him.

We were able to get Allen to do many things which helped him to gain some confidence in himself, but it was uphill, trying to get the school to cooperate. The teacher and the principal both agreed that inasmuch as Allen was in the sixth grade he should use sixth-grade materials. Dumb! So in his out-of-school classes he read successfully from third-grade level books, but had to go to the sixth-grade level in school despite the fact that he could not master those at all. However, at the end of the school year, the principal agreed to let him go on to the seventh grade, which made a new man out of Allen. He still needed additional help, but at least he was moving about with a little bit of ego in him now.

Ah, these kids we hurt; these kids we knock down and step on in our progressive schools. Speaking of Allen makes me remember Jeff. Jeff was not like Allen, at least in one way. Jeff was in the eighth grade and large for his age. Well, maybe he wasn't large for his age, but he was large for his grade. He had been retained two years in the second grade. Early in the summer of his fourteenth year, his mother came to me with Jeff's story. Before she told me about him she asked me if I would take another patient. I said no, that I was filled up for the summer, but she began to cry. I just never was any good against a woman's tears, especially those of a mother's. So I agreed to listen to her story. Here it is briefly.

Jeff had just completed the eighth grade but was now slated for the special education class next September. He had been tested by the school psychologist and found to be just what several of his teachers had suspected; mentally retarded. He had an I.Q., they said, of less than 78, and his teachers were glad to get him off their hands. But his mother said he certainly had never acted like a mentally retarded person at home. He could do things that everybody else could do, except at school, where it seemed he just couldn't do well. She insisted that he was not a fit subject for special education, and would I please at least test him, even if I couldn't work with him later on. I finally said yes, but that she should also have him given a complete physical examination including an eye test. She said ok.

Over the next three weeks I administered three tests to him: Wechsler Intelligence Test for Children (WISC), the Stanford-Binet, and the Stencil Design Test. He scored 98, 100, and 96 respectively, on those three tests. Retarded? Not according to those tests. The mother, of course, was almost out of her mind with joy. In the meantime, she had made arrangements for a physical examination, which he was given. They found that his tonsils were very bad and should be removed. In due time they were.

I also tested his reading. One of the people on my staff had been working with him for a week on his reading and reported to me that the boy was able to carry on a very intelligent conversation, etc., but that he *did* read in a very peculiar manner. She said that as he read he would keep jerking his head in an odd way, as though trying to see the words with just one eye. So I checked his reading and sure enough, he seemed to be trying to look *back* with one eye at what he had just read. It was more than passing strange. Meanwhile he had been tested some fifty miles away by a trained eye specialist. His mother reported the following very interesting experience.

The eye doctor had tested the boy and began swearing in a loud tone of voice. He asked the boy how long he had been wearing his glasses and the boy and the mother both agreed that it had been since he was in second grade, but that the lenses had been changed from time to time by their local eye specialist. The doctor swore again, exclaiming that he would like to get his hands on that quack. You see, for six years at least that boy had been wearing the lens in the *right* spectacle that was designed for the *left* spectacle and *vice versa*. No wonder the boy read in such a peculiar manner. No wonder he was classed as mentally retarded.

Both anger and joy reigned in that household that night. The I.Q. test results, and now this, were almost too much for them. They were extremely grateful, but would we continue working with him? And what should they do about that school psychologist and his report to the superintendent? Would Jeff still have to go to the special education class? And what about that eye doctor who had prescribed wrongly for six years? And what about those teachers who never suspected anything, and never did anything to help the boy? Why had they not referred him years ago for some special attention? All of these why's and what's. I didn't blame them a bit. I wanted to stamp on a bunch of people myself. I did write a complete report and sent it to the superintendent of schools. He agreed that Jeff should not be placed in the special class, and that he would need some special attention for some time in order to bring him up to grade level. Anyway, things were looking up for Jeff, for the first time in years.

Cruel and inhuman punishment. That's what I saw one day when I went into a classroom to observe. It was a fourth grade, and they were having a Valentine Day's party. Most of the kids were gathered around the teacher's desk while the valentines were being passed out. Two of the youngsters were calling out the names of the others as the valentines were taken out of the box. It looked as though they were having a gay time, all right. But there was one that was not, and it was pretty darned obvious. She was sitting by herself near the back of the room and over to one side—crying. I couldn't help but notice her, but didn't go to her at that time. The student teacher saw me and came smilingly toward me. She seemed quite happy with the way things were going.

We talked for a bit and she told me what was going on. Then I asked her about the crying girl. Immediately she saddened and glancing over her shoulder in the direction of the teacher's desk, she whispered that the girl, Sally, was being punished by the teacher for not having done her work. It seems that lately the child's usual good work had fallen off, and the teacher was trying to "bring her to heel." She had threatened to take some serious measures before, and now was carrying out her threat *by refusing to allow the child to get her valentines until she brought up her work,* or at least finished the assignments in which she was behind! So Sally was working and crying at the same time. But no valentines yet.

I gave the student teacher the devil for not going to bat for Sally, and she promised to do so. When the supervising teacher had a free minute, I talked with her about the student teacher's work, and she glowed with enthusiasm about the things the young teacher was doing—and learning, even. Then I asked her about Sally, which really was not my business to do. I was there to observe the student teacher only; but the supervising teacher told me very righteously that Sally was being punished, and what for, and how.

I felt like hitting that teacher. I didn't: I couldn't. The institution for which I was working would have been in hot water, and so would I! But I did suggest that this was rather an unusual kind of punishment, at which the teacher replied that she believed in being firm with the children because many of them just didn't get the right kind of training at home. No doubt the latter part of her statement was true, but the teacher's main job is not to punish. Too many of our teachers spend too much time on punitive activities, liking to think of themselves as "good disciplinarians." Faugh! And bah, too! The really good disciplinarians in our schools are those who are doing such a good job of teaching that punishment is the last thing they think of. They don't need it.

But about Sally. The student teacher told me on my next visit to her that they had discovered why Sally's work had fallen off so. It seems that her mother had been in the hospital for three weeks, and that Sally and her sixth-grade sister had been at home alone during that time. When asked where their father was, the sixth-grade sister had replied sadly, "We don't know. We haven't seen Daddy for a long time." The welfare authorities were notified immediately.

But why hadn't that stupid teacher had the sense to try to find out why Sally's work had gone down? On one occasion when I was talking to her about some other things, she pointed out to me that she had twenty-eight pupils in her room, and that she didn't have time to work with every child individually. Well, blast her right out of the classroom. I don't want anyone like her teaching *my* children. And you don't want her teaching *yours*.

Did you know that there are about 3 million schoolchildren today, this very day, who are being taught by such teachers as Sally's? And we are standing by letting them get away with it. That's one of the reasons for this book. We need to organize some Raiders and get rid of these teachers. This means doing away with a lot of tenure laws, of course, but that is not impossible. We just have to begin putting pressure on school systems, both state and local. If enough parents read this book we'll get some things done. Whoever said that our schools are "factories of futility" knew exactly what he was talking about. We need to organize some legal raids on the schools and throw out the criminal teachers, the Sally's teachers, for example.

I have another Valentine Day's story. Julia was a little Mexican girl who was very shy. So shy, in fact, that she seldom spoke even to the other kids in the room. One of the reasons for it was that she did not speak English well. In her home Mexican was spoken, and Julia had not learned to speak English in school as her teachers wanted her to speak. So the less she spoke, the less she learned, and the less she learned, the shyer she became. As a result of this and the fact that she was a Mexican and lived in "Chili Town," Julia was a shy and forgotten third-grader on Valentine's Day.

As in the case of Sally above, the valentines were being passed out and there was much excitement in the room. The girl across the aisle from Julia was getting a whole stack of valentines, and on Julia's desk there was none. It was beginning to look mighty obvious. Then the valentine box was empty, and so was Julia's heart. She had not even received one from the teacher! She had not received one from *anybody!* One of the kids in the room, as kids will, not meaning to be cruel, said to the class in general: "Hey look, Julia didn't get any valentines."

Julia looked stunned and embarrassed. She sat with her head down, looking the other way. Then she burst into tears and ran from the room.

Again, cruel and inhuman punishment. Why wasn't Julia's teacher alert to the situation? Who was on Julia's side? She wanted to be a *third-grade* dropout. Who can blame her?

We make some of the most dastardly mistakes in our schools. Maybe that's because we have nearly two hundred thousand teachers who should not be in the schools, and whom we should get rid of. One of the sorriest practices we have is that of retaining a child who has not been doing well in his class. We seem to think that if we hold him back in this manner, his problem will be solved. Well, we hold him back, all right. Way back. Nearly every study of any note shows that retaining a child in a grade for a second year does him no good whatever, and often does him considerable harm. Go into any schoolroom and be told that there are two or three kids in there who are repeating that grade. Then ask if they are the top students. What a laugh! They are usually at the *bottom* of the class. Oh, there are a few exceptions, as there are to any rule, but they *are* exceptions. Think back to Allen of this chapter. He had been retained in kindergarten, but he was still among the lowest in his class all through school. He was even going to be retained again, according to his nincompoop of a teacher.

But another case in point is Manuel. He was named Manuel but he was called "Manwell" by the whites in his town. He was a Mexican also, and like Julia, he lived in "Chili Town." This meant that it didn't make a whole lot of difference whether he got along well in school or not. He was in the second grade and doing poorly. Just why he was doing poorly no one seemed to know really. He didn't know how to read worth a darn, according to his white teacher. The reason for that was obvious enough to the teachers, i.e., he was Mexican. No other reason was needed. His teacher talked it over with the principal, who had no more interest than the teacher, and apparently knew even less than she about *why* Manwell was not doing second-grade work.

It was decided that they would put Manwell back to the

first grade, assuming that it was all right with the first-grade teacher—not the same teacher he had had the year before, but with one who was new this year. It was all right with her, too. So one afternoon just before time for school to let out, his second-grade teacher told Manwell to get all of his papers and put them together, and to bring to her all of his books. Manwell didn't know what was going on. (Neither did the stupid teachers, really.)

Then Mrs. B. called Manwell up to her desk, took him by the arm and led him out into the hallway. There she put her hand tenderly on his shoulder, and with great compassion in her voice, told him that he was being put back to the first grade. Manwell looked at her with his big brown eyes full of tears, and *shook*. He literally trembled all over. This was the first indication he had had that he was to be demoted. There had been no communication between the school and the parents concerning Manwell's work. The parents knew nothing of the demotion.

How mean and low-down can people get? Teachers, I mean. And school principals too!

Manwell was speechless as his teacher led him to the first-grade room. There he was met by the first-grade teacher who led him into the room and to his desk. She explained briefly that Manwell would be joining them. Of course, all of the kids already knew him. They all played together outside. Now they knew that Manwell was being "put back." It meant the end of life to Manwell, at least for several days. How would *you* like to be demoted right in front of your friends and acquaintances? None of us would like it, even if we deserved it. But Manwell was only a little Mexican kid. He didn't have any feelings. Just tears. Just trembling. Just heartbreak. Just a lousy teacher who was inefficient and lazy, and a school principal on the same level.

DTSS—FSA!

A poem comes to mind. I don't believe it has a title, and the author is unknown. It's very fitting right here, I believe.

A sad-faced little fellow sits alone in deep disgrace;

There's a lump arising in his throat, and tears drop down
  his face.
He wandered from his playmates; he doesn't want to hear
Their shouts of merry laughter since the world has lost its
  cheer.
He has sipped the cup of sorrow; he has quaffed the bitter
  glass
And his heart is fairly breaking—the boy who didn't pass.

In the apple tree the robin sings a cheery little song,
But he doesn't seem to hear it, showing plainly something's
  wrong.
Comes his faithful little spaniel for a romp and bit of play,
But the troubled little fellow bids him sternly "go away!"
And alone he sits in sorrow with his hair a tangled mass
And his eyes are red from weeping—the boy who didn't pass.

Oh, you who boast a laughing son, and speak of him as
  bright,
And you, who love a little girl who comes to you at night
With shining eyes and dancing feet with honors from her
  school,
Turn to that lonely lad who thinks he is a fool,
And take him kindly by the hand, the dullest in the class,
He is the one who most needs help—

The Little Boy who didn't pass!
A note of reminder to teachers: The Master said to "suffer
the little children." He didn't say to *make* them suffer.

A while back a mother called me on the long distance telephone at midnight. Her first words were: "Mike says he's going
to commit suicide."

What does one say at a time like that, and in those circumstances? So I gave out with an intelligent "Oh? Why?" And
she told me this story. The eighth-grade teacher that day had
asked the kids to write down the names of their classmates in
two lists. In one list they were to put the ones they liked, and

tell why. In the other they were to put the ones they didn't like, and tell why. Then the teacher collected the lists and one by one called the students up to his desk and showed them the results. Not one person had listed Mike's name on the "like" list. Nearly everyone had him on their "dislike" list. And that teacher showed this to Mike.

Will someone please tell me how anyone could be so downright stupid as that? Mike was hurt beyond measure. No wonder he said he was going to commit suicide. If nobody wanted him around, why should he stay around? This was exactly what he said to his mother. It almost made sense, didn't it? It certainly did as far as Mike was concerned. And that teacher had been hired to act like a blasted fool, apparently. He was one of those tenured teachers and hard to fire. The tenure laws protect witless teachers. That's another reason why we need to make a raid on the schools. We need to round up some of these dopes like Mike's teacher and put them out of the Kid's Prison so it'll stop being a prison.

As it turned out, Mike didn't commit suicide. His mother talked with the teacher and told him what he had done to Mike. The teacher was sorry, and said he would make it right with Mike. But the damage had been done. Mike would never be the same. He was quite short in stature, was a good kid, but just didn't know how to act around people. Now he was even more unsure of himself. That teacher really *did* know how to hurt a guy.

Robert was thirteen years old and had never been in any one school more than three weeks at a time. No school wanted him. They said that he was obstreperous, rude, crude, and probably mentally retarded. He cursed the teachers as well as the kids. No school person wanted anything to do with him. In the summer of his thirteenth year the director of a day camp for the mentally handicapped was finally persuaded by the mother to accept him there on a trial basis. The director then asked me if I would be willing to let Robert try some reading exercises from time to time. (I was holding classes next door to the day camp.) I agreed, especially inasmuch as the director and I were using several of the same exercises for developing the brain.

The first morning Robert came he walked right up to me, stuck out his hand, and greeted me very politely. For the next six weeks he gave me no trouble whatever. Indeed, he made such progress in reading that I asked him to appear on a television show with me so that he could demonstrate his reading ability. You see, from practically a nonreader, Robert had progressed up to five-hundred words a minute and was able to give a fair-to-good account of what he read. It was a proud day for Robert. This was the first time he had ever gained the respectful attention of any audience. Always before, any attention he had gained was one of frowns and strong admonitions. He performed well on TV, and was even asked if he would like to try it again.

What was it that had happened to Robert? And why hadn't some teachers and psychologists discovered the basic causes of his problems? Was his case like those of the school psychologist in a large school system who told me about his work? He said he could test a child, but he didn't know what to tell the teachers to do.That certainly seemed to be the case with Robert. Again, as I think of his situation, I find myself wanting to throw vivid curses at the stupid fools who caused Robert and his parents eight years of tears and worry.

I tested Robert for mixed dominance among other things, and found him to be more left-sided than right-sided. When I reported my findings to his parents they laughed sort of help-lessly, and said that three psychologists had tested him and decided that he should be *right*-sided. I tested him again and found him as I had before, and so told his parents. My findings were reported to the school authorities, and they agreed to have Robert tested again by one of *their* psychologists. One did test him, and found him to be more left-sided than right. In the meantime, I had already begun Robert on a series of exercises designed to strengthen his left-sidedness, even to carrying his right arm in a sling part of the day. Crazy? Well, maybe so. But *something* began to happen within Robert.

I can't take all the credit, certainly. His camp director had him creeping on his hands and knees with the other children several times a day, and his parents encouraged him in his reading practice daily. There were other exercises that we had him go through every day, and Robert began to respond. He would come proudly to class and greet everybody cheerfully and somewhat loudly, but no one minded very much. He was always respectful, and only once did he swear out loud, then immediately apologized. The day I asked him to take part on the TV show he declared to be the happiest day of his life. It was only equaled by the day of the actual presentation.

That was in the late summer. At Christmastime I received a card from his mother; one of the most meaningful cards I have ever received. It merely said: "Robert is in the seventh grade and is making A's and B's. He loves school." Robert, you see, had arrived. It was the first time in eight years of Kids' Prison that it had been anything but that for him. It was the first time he had even been allowed to stay in a school long enough for him to show what he could do.

You teachers who create factories of futility for the children, get up off your seats of learning and earn your pay for a change.

Speaking of left-sidedness, I must tell you about Rodney. I didn't meet him until he was in the fifth grade, and I was almost sorry that I did then. I say that because every time I think of him, I want to slap a woman teacher as hard as I can. Not just *any* woman teacher, you understand; just Rodney's, in this case. When he was in the first grade he had as his teacher an old maid who had taught far too long, and probably should never have been allowed in the classroom. She was a stickler for neatness. She required the children to turn their papers a certain direction when they wrote because, she said, she wanted to maintain a neat room. Nothing out of order. Certainly not the kids' papers. But comes Rodney, and she encountered a problem.

Rodney was left-handed and wanted to turn his paper like most left-handers do when they write. But that meant getting his paper out of line. It destroyed the neat setup of the room, and the teacher took steps. She made Rodney turn his paper just like the rest of the class. When her back was turned, however, Rodney would shift his paper back the way *he* wanted it. This the teacher would not countenance. She put Rodney in the broom closet as punishment. She said he would stay there until he could learn to behave.

It happened that Rodney was dreadfully afraid of the dark, and that closet was dark. He screamed and screamed. She let him out on the condition that he would hold his paper "in the right way." He promised, and kept his promise until the teacher wasn't looking, then turned it back so that he could write comfortably. The teacher caught him at it, and back to the broom closet he went.

This kind of thing went on throughout the school year. When it came time to promote or not to promote, Rodney was not. When he learned of it he set up a dreadful howl. His parents understood. They moved into another district away from that tyrant. But damage had been done that would take years to correct. That damnable teacher was the cause of Rodney's failing, and of having to go to a psychiatrist once a week for several years. She had caused emotional damage that would last a long time.

And to think that we pay such teachers for committing mental and emotional mayhem on our children! In the fifth grade Rodney was a very poor reader, and had several blocks which we had to take down carefully and slowly. What had taken years to build up within Rodney was sure to be slow to come out, but we felt progress was being made when his mother reported that, "Rodney has finally decided that reading can be fun." That was the first thing we had worked toward.

The story doesn't end exactly there. Quite by coincidence, Rodney's first-grade teacher came to see me one day late in August. She did not come by appointment, but "just dropped in" to see me about something. It seems that her school board had decided to put in a special reading program in the school, and they had asked her to be the special reading teacher! Well, shiver my timbers! I wanted to hang her from the yard arm by her heels. Then she really "busted me wide open." She looked at her watch, and said to me, "Would you tell me all you can about remedial reading, please? I don't have much time. My husband is supposed to pick me up in fifteen minutes." Well, blast her sorry little heart.

You raiders; let's start with *her!*

Morning Sickness in the First Grade. You mothers are all familiar with morning sickness, but did you know that literally thousands of first-graders have it too, and sometimes for more than three months? The other day a mother came to see me about her first-grade boy. She was about the umpteenth one to tell me this story. Her son gets sick at his stomach every day before going to school. Sometimes she suspects that he is not sick, but faking it. In any event, he doesn't want to go to school. Sometimes he actually throws up, becomes violently ill. The mother went to see his teacher and the principal. Both of them felt sorry for little Troy, and promised to try to help him. "But," said the mother, "why does he become ill every morning? What happens at school that makes him not want to go?"

The teacher assured Troy's mother that she loved him, and treated him kindly. "Of course," remarked the teacher, "he *is* having some trouble with his reading, and I've placed him in the lowest group just to give him confidence." The effortless stupidity of some teachers is truly overwhelming. Who ever gained confidence by having his ego knocked down?

There were further inquiries by the mother. It seems that the teacher had *five* reading groups in her room. Now, that's pretty good isn't it? Most teachers have only three. But you know what? *All five of the groups were using the same set of readers and workbooks.* At the request of the mother I visited that teacher's room. I saw a huge stack of opened workbooks on her desk. A discreet inquiry (at least *I* thought it was discreet) brought forth the information that the teacher would grade those things while the children were at recess. Then when they returned they would have another go at them. I thought to myself that just the sight of those workbooks would be enough to make me sick. And I could read them. More's the pity.

As I observed in that room I learned why it was that Troy could become ill every morning. That teacher insisted that every child read aloud from the textbook in his particular circle. The best readers in the class did fine. Some of them even seemed to enjoy the process, but not Troy's group. His group had to read the same tripe that the top group was reading, and kids in his group couldn't read the stuff. The teacher had a long pointer stick or rod and when a child made a mistake, she would poke him or tap him with it. Troy got poked several times while I was there. Each time he would look embarrassed and his face would change color.

Now, people, I've got to stop talking about it, because as I relive that experience I want to trample that teacher into the earth. That's where she belongs. Way down deep in the Devil's Pit. And if you don't agree with me already, I'll bet you will when you hear this: After my visit there, and in a discussion with Troy's mother, she told me that her husband had told her just the night before that *he* had had Old Lady J. as *his* first-grade teacher twenty-five years before, and *he* got sick several mornings when it came time to go to school. She had "scared the pants off me," Troy's father told his mother.

You'd have thought, would you not, that the school would have long since gotten rid of that teacher. But you are wrong. The day that I went to visit that room, the principal, from whom I obtained permission to visit, told me that Mrs. J. was one of his finest teachers, "and the best first-grade teacher in our entire school system," he declared.

Old Lady J. had been teaching there for at least twenty-five years in that same room. How many helpless children did she destroy? How many ulcers did she help to develop in kids? Troy's father had some; his wife told me. That teacher held sway in her kids' Prison Room.

Anyway, do you understand why we have to form a group of Raiders (or Ridders) and rid the schools of the hundred thousand or more menaces now confronting our children? These menaces are hurting not only the hurt kids, but also holding back the learning of all others.

Chapter XI

Unfettering the Fettered

(*The Blind, the Deaf, the Retarted*)

We have the world of the Fettered around us. But even as I write this, some remarkable things are happening in this world of the Fettered. Maybe the people in that world are becoming a little less so. A blind college girl is reading two-thousand words a minute in braille. A deaf and dumb man is reading eight-thousand words a minute. A mentally retarded high school girl is reading more than one-thousand words a minute. Sounds like progress.

"Ah," you say, "I don't believe in that speed reading business." Okay, don't believe it. Then you'll make all the blind people who read braille continue to read at a rate of 90 to 110 words a minute. Do you know what that's like? Let me tell you. An average-sighted second-grader (that's a second-grader who can see all right) reads faster than a blind adult who reads braille. Or look at it this way. A blind person reads about as fast as you or I would read if we were looking through a funnel at the words but were able to see only one or two letters of each word at a time. Then you or I would be reading about 95 to 110 words a minute. We would indeed feel chained, wouldn't we? But you don't believe in speed reading. Then you and the blind person and the second-grader must continue to read at 90 to 110 words a minute. You can really learn that way, can't you?

Actually, you read at about 250 to 300 words a minute. For a blind person, that would be awfully fast, but you're not willing to let him read that fast, are you? You don't believe in speed reading. You would also limit the mentally retarded person in much the same way. For him, a rate of 300 would be speed reading. How about that? Are you selfish or something? Or just scared? I mean, are you actually afraid that you can't

152

do any better? Well, let me reassure you. If you are a young person who hasn't learned too much, you *can* do better. But if you are one of those smart adults, and especially if you are a reading expert who has written books about reading, then you are indeed lost. There's not much hope for you because you won't try. There is none so *trying* as he who will not try. (Hey, I just made that up. It's pretty good, huh?)

Now, about teaching these fettered retarded to read faster; it can be done. But it cannot be done if you have the attitude that many educators have. They (the educators) seem really determined to keep these kids from having their chance. Even the experts in the field of special education have not yet got around to thinking about this idea of having the mentally retarded read any faster than about 80 to 100 words a minute. Let's keep them fettered, they seem to be saying. Okay, maybe they don't say that, but their actions certainly indicate that because they neglect to put anything of the kind in the stuff they write.

But we know they can do much more than we have previously allowed them. Again I must refer to this erroneous philosophy that many seem to have concerning learning. It says that if a person is lacking in something, give him small doses of what he is lacking in and he will get well. Hogwash, poppycock, and stuff like that! We should give them huge doses to get them well. That's what we did with a bunch of kids who were classed as mentally retarded, and they responded nobly. Here's the story.

We worked with twenty-seven children who had been classed as mentally retarded. They ranged in chronological age from seven and one-half years to fifteen years. In I.Q., as determined from the WISC, they ranged from a low of 64 to a high of 98. Obviously, they were not all retarded as usually defined, but their work in school was such that the school felt that they were in a lower category. Anyway, we had them "given" to us as mentally retarded. Because of irregularities in the school calendar, we had some of them for eight weeks and the others for twelve weeks. We met with them daily for forty to sixty minutes, depending on recess periods, gym periods, band periods, and other interruptions.

We began teaching these kids the principles of rapid reading, using as much as possible materials that were on their grade levels. It was sometimes difficult to get materials that some of them could read, and we had to resort to preschool-level books. This made it even more difficult because such books have too many pictures in them to be good for this purpose. We wanted them to encounter thousands of words daily, not just a few on a page or two or three, as was the usual custom. You might say that we were giving children giant doses of what they were lacking, and they began to respond, slowly at first, then more rapidly. Some jumped way out ahead of the others; some responded like snails. But all were eager for the special teachers to come in and start "those crazy reading classes," as some of the kids called them.

I won't go into detail on the precise methods and techniques used, because I did that in an earlier chapter. It is important to note, however, that we treated each child as an individual in the way he saw, the way he wanted to hold his book, the position in which he sat (or stood), and what he read. He could read anything he chose as long as he and we made sure that he was able to read it easily. We told them that we didn't care how easy the stuff was, but we'd get real mad at them if they were trying to read something that was too hard. The kids had fun and so did the teachers. It was supposed to be a fun time, not a serious and solemn time like many class periods are.

Let's see what happened. I'm going to deal in averages now, realizing that sometimes they don't mean much, but this is just to give an idea of what can be done, of some of the great possibilities which are before us. The average reading rate of these twenty-seven children was 83 words per minute when we started the special program. Their average comprehension was 56 percent. The lowest reading rate in the beginning was 25 wpm, and the lowest single comprehension score was 30 percent. The highest rate in wpm in the beginning was 131, and the highest comprehension score was 74 percent.

On the final testing of these children, the average reading rate of the twenty-seven was 489 wpm, with an average comprehension score of 68. You can see that they made a tremendous gain in rate, and at the same time went up 12 percent in comprehension. The slowest reader at the end of the program read 51 wpm, but this was an increase of 100 percent over what he had been reading earlier. But his comprehension had gone from 62 to 88 percent!

The fastest single reader at the end of the program had shot up to 1,455 wpm, with a comprehension score of 83. Her original rate had been 89 wpm, with 74 percent comprehension.

As I said above, averages sometimes mean little, but individual scores often mean a great deal. These scores show that mentally retarded children are capable of doing much more than we have allowed them to do. If we really want to help them we'd better "get on the stick" and give them a chance to show what they can do. We are actually damning them when we hold them back as we usually do in the classrooms in special education. These children whose scores I have been talking about hadn't known that there were other possibilities for them. Most of them responded with great enthusiasm to the whole idea. They seemed actually to want to be challenged. Who wouldn't want to get away from the drudgery that most of them have to go through in their classrooms? They have to humdrum their way through loads and loads of workbooks and work sheets each year, never knowing the challenge of swift thinking and responding.

There are two boys, ages thirteen and fifteen, in Maryland, who are whizzes in reading. Both were classed as mentally retarded. Yet both read one thousand words a minute or more, and both thoroughly enjoy doing it. One of them is now in junior high school and making such grades that he almost made the honor roll there last semester. What do we mean when we say that these kids can't achieve like other people in school? I can tell you this: they never will as long as we think they can't and don't give them the chance to try.

What about other things for these kids? How about math and spelling? The same thing applies. We need to give them more and more of what they need, not less. Again, it seems so dumb of us to give them very small doses of what they are lacking when it's more that they need; more math, more spelling, more reading, more of the skills in which they are short. Now, I didn't say more *pressure* on them. That we can do without, for the most part anyway. A little bit of pressure is sometimes a good thing, but we do have to be careful about that. I'm talking about the same kind of thing we have done with so-called normal kids in math and spelling, for example, where we've given them several hundred math problems and spelling words and had them work them in a very short period of time. They love the challenge. The slower youngsters might not get as many of them right, or even do as many of them, but think how many *more* they will encounter and think how many more they will get right than if they had just a few to do. Think how much more they will learn this way than they would with just a few problems, or spelling words, or reading books.

And just think how much more pure enjoyment the kids will get from the challenges. There is so very little that is truly challenging in the lives of these kinds of pupils. We can lift them way up if we will. But again, we have to want to, and have sense enough to do it.

I must tell you about Nancy. She is the first blind person to read faster than a few hundred words a minute. Remember that the average blind person reads at about 95 to 110 words a minute. This is terribly slow, of course. Until recently it was thought that this was about as much as a blind person could do, but our Nancy has proved otherwise. She has been able to throw off some of the fetters that have bound her. She, at this writing, reads rather comfortably at a little over two thousand words a minute with excellent comprehension.

She uses the index fingers of both hands reading across the page halfway with her left forefinger, then completing the line with her right forefinger. As the right hand moves on across the page, the left is going back to begin the next line of raised dots. Her hands move swiftly an dsmoothly in a beautiful and synchronized manner. Her main difficulty is in turning the pages. Braille books have much larger pages than the print books, and it takes longer to turn the pages. It actually takes her about one and a half seconds to turn a page, which means that in one minute of reading, she loses approximately 165 words. That is more than twice as many words as many blind people read in a minute, and is as many as some sighted adults read in print.

Nancy is a college senior majoring in music. Twice she rejected the idea of attempting to experiment with rapid reading. She said she was sure it could not be done. More than two years after the first suggestion, she agreed to the experiment. Now we all regret that we had to wait that long. You see, it is truly amazing what the human mind is capable of doing once it has tried something. Nancy was convinced that it was impossible. Now she has accomplished that impossible and is heading for faster speeds.

I must point out that in all this talk of speed, it is not speed just for the sake of speed for which we are working. That would be foolish indeed. But rather it is what that speeded-up process does for us. It enables us to learn tons more, and to enjoy life immeasurably more. And it saves gobs and gobs of time. Nancy, for example, spends far less time now in braille reading than she did previously, yet reads a great deal more material. We might compare it this way: While the average braille person is reading one book, Nancy can read twenty. Or, while the average sighted person is reading one print book, Nancy can read eight to ten braille books.

From being extremely doubtful about its possibilities, Nancy is now considering teaching other blind students to read rapidly while she is attending graduate school. In the meantime, the American Foundation for the Blind and various state schools for the blind are becoming interested, and already have made arrangements to visit us and see for themselves this "miracle" which has transpired. "Miracle" was the expression used by an official of the AFB. I think we all believe that it may well be one of the real breakthroughs in achieving independent living for the blind.

A short time ago I was sitting in La Guardia Airport in New York when a woman walked in and began distributing little cards on which was printed certain information about her. The cards said that she was a deaf mute, the mother of four children, etc. It was sad, truly sad. This experience was brought to mind again when I returned to my place of work and had an interview with one of my college seniors who is working part time with a group of deaf children. The student told me that one of the pupils with whom she was working, a child ten years of age, had been taught to read and to speak. Her speaking, apparently, was only fair, and her reading was even less than that. That seemed strange until my student told me more about the young girl.

The teaching of these children is very slow, she said. The teaching of math, for example, is a tedious process, composed mostly of games. Now, this may be a good way of entertaining children, but it is not the fastest way to teach them very much. This kind of thing we have been doing for years and years with all kinds of children. It has not brought us many outstanding successes. We are not a nation noted for its masses of mathematicians, just as we don't have masses of excellent readers, nor even good readers; nor spellers. We cling to these methods which have not proved successful, and continue to have mediocre results. The woman passing out the cards was a product of these methods. Others with similiar handicaps have gone further, no doubt, and have accomplished more. But we always have exceptions. It's the nonexceptions that I'm worried about.

We really do some crazy thinking. Stupid, that is. Irrational. Of necessity, deaf persons learn most of what they know by seeing and reading. They have to depend upon their reading to gain much of their information. Yet what do we do? We do some more damning. We stop them, pull them up short. We cut them off right at the source of their learning supply. Let me show you what I mean.

A few years ago I had occasion to work with a group of deaf adults in a class in rapid reading. One of the group was an official in the American Association for the Deaf. At the beginning of the course, not one of those adults could read more than three hundred words a minute. Most of them read less than two hundred words a minute. (You see, they were doubly fettered.) I wanted to know why this was so. Gradually it came out that in their early training in reading in the various schools which they attended, they had all had about the same kinds of reading experiences. They had been taught slowly and laboriously, therefore they had learned that way. They had learned to read slowly and tediously, word by word, all through their school years and they were still reading the same way. Again, their principal source of learning had been like a shallow well. It had produced little because there was little there. Their source was too dry.

It was a case again of where little is given, little is learned. They had been taught a few words a day, therefore they had learned only a few. Yet these people were the ones who had needed more than anyone else to have many given them. It was to be their best way of learning. Once more as I consider this situation, I am struck by the enormity of our irrationality. Why have we not been able to see this before? Why is it that many of us are still of the opinion that what we have done for these fettered is all that we could have done?

Recently I was talking with the principal of a public school in which there are special classes for the deaf and for those with partial hearing losses. He told me that he was very proud of the progress the kids in these classes were making. But when I visited the classes in that school and saw the same approaches being used with these particular handicapped children that we had used eighteen years earlier in a school in Virginia, I felt like weeping. Oh, there were some improvements of course, in some of the equipment and materials, and even in some of the kinds of treatment afforded them, but in this all-important form of communication of reading, the approaches were ancient and should have been obsolete. They had not produced, and still do not produce, the results we want and need. This form of communication for the deaf must be a highly refined and successful method if they are to approach the independent living that we all desire and deserve.

In the rapid reading course for the deaf that I was speaking about, we did not give them a few pages a day to read, along with a few pages of workbook stuff. (Workbooks are mostly stuff and nonsense, anyway.) Rather, we gave them dozens and hundreds of pages of material to go through. We showed them how to do this, but with each one discovering and developing his own best techniques of seeing. In the process, we discovered something of great interest to us and, we believe, of real significance in teaching the deaf and hard of hearing to read: Those who have been deaf since birth or from an early age have less difficulty discontinuing saying the words in their minds as they read than do we of the hearing world. We latter have been taught to say each word in our minds. As a result, most of us read slowly because we "talk" our way across a page.

It is different with many of the deaf people. They are able to bypass one step in learning to read really well. Since they do not subvocalize, as we call it, they can learn much faster and much more quickly than many of us who hear normally. If the teachers of deaf children were to recognize and take advantage of this peculiarity the unfettering process in the area of reading would be hurried up, and a lot of people would be a lot happier. The members of my deaf class in reading went from an average speed of less than 200 words per minute to an average rate of 1380 words a minute. The highest score was made by a man who had been deaf from birth. His reading rate was nearly 8,000 words a minute, with what we call "book report" comprehension. The lowest score was made by a woman who also had been deaf all of her life. She read 750 words a minute also with good comprehension. Even at her "slow" rate of reading, she could go through about three books while the average hearing person goes through one.

There are all kinds of fettered persons around us. A cerebral palsied man, severely brain-damaged at birth, and whose speech is labored and unclear, neverthless can read from 3,000 to 5,000 words a minute with good comprehension. He could read faster but he has much difficulty turning the pages because of his handicap. Who would ever have thought that such a one as he could perform in so excellent a manner? Certainly not the people where he went to school: they did a fine thing for him and with him.

But there are far, far better things for us to do than we have yet done. We have but to pick up the challenge!